First World War

and Army of Occupation

War Diary

France, Belgium and Germany

18 DIVISION
53 Infantry Brigade,
Brigade Machine Gun Company
9 February 1916 - 31 December 1917

WO95/2040/3

The Naval & Military Press Ltd
www.nmarchive.com
Published in association with The National Archives

Published by

The Naval & Military Press Ltd

Unit 10 Ridgewood Industrial Park,

Uckfield, East Sussex,

TN22 5QE England

Tel: +44 (0) 1825 749494

www.naval-military-press.com

www.nmarchive.com

This diary has been reprinted in facsimile from the original. Any imperfections are inevitably reproduced and the quality may fall short of modern type and cartographic standards.

Contents

Document type	Place/Title	Date From	Date To
Heading	WO 2040/3		
Heading	18th Division 53rd Mach. Gun Coy. Feb 1916-Dec 1917		
Heading	War Diary 53rd Machine Gun Company. Feb 9-Feb 28 March 1-March 31 1916		
War Diary	Havre	09/02/1916	12/02/1916
War Diary	Albert	13/02/1916	02/03/1916
War Diary	Franvillers	03/03/1916	14/03/1916
War Diary	Etinehem	15/03/1916	15/03/1916
War Diary	Bray	16/03/1916	31/03/1916
Heading	War Diary 53rd Coy Machine Gun Corps April 1916		
War Diary	Bray	01/04/1916	30/04/1916
Miscellaneous	From O.C. 53 M.G. Coy D.A.G 3rd Echelon.	02/06/1916	02/06/1916
Heading	War Diary For Month of May 1916 53rd Company Machine Gun Corps Vol 3		
War Diary	Sally Laurette	01/05/1916	01/05/1916
War Diary	Daours	02/05/1916	02/05/1916
War Diary	Longpre	03/05/1916	04/05/1916
War Diary	Ailly-Sur-Somme	05/05/1916	23/05/1916
War Diary	Corbie	24/05/1916	24/05/1916
War Diary	Bray	25/05/1916	31/05/1916
Miscellaneous	From O.C. 53 M.G.M.	06/08/1916	06/08/1916
Heading	War Diary June 1916 53rd Machine Gun Company Vol 4		
War Diary	Bray	01/06/1916	11/06/1916
War Diary	Southy-Le-Sec	12/06/1916	16/06/1916
War Diary	Bray	17/06/1916	24/06/1916
War Diary	Grovetown	24/06/1916	30/06/1916
Heading	53rd Bde. 18th Div. 53rd Machine Gun Company. July 1916 Battle of the Somme		
Heading	War Diary For Month Of July 1916 53 M G Coy		
War Diary	Carnoy	01/07/1916	07/07/1916
War Diary	Bronfay Farm	08/07/1916	08/07/1916
War Diary	Grovetown	09/07/1916	14/07/1916
War Diary	Billon Valley	14/07/1916	14/07/1916
War Diary	Maricourt	14/07/1916	19/07/1916
War Diary	Montauban	19/07/1916	19/07/1916
War Diary	Montauban (Longueval)	19/07/1916	21/07/1916
War Diary	Grovetown	22/07/1916	22/07/1916
War Diary	Train	22/07/1916	22/07/1916
War Diary	Longpre (Sur Somme)	22/07/1916	24/07/1916
War Diary	Blairinghem	25/07/1916	29/07/1916
War Diary	Godwaers Weld	30/07/1916	31/07/1916
War Diary	Carnoy-Montaubon	01/07/1916	01/07/1916
War Diary	Carnoy-Montaubon	24/06/1916	24/06/1916
War Diary	Carnoy-Montaubon	08/07/1916	08/07/1916
War Diary	Longueval Delville Wood	19/07/1916	22/07/1916
Miscellaneous	From O.C. 53 M.G. Coy. To 53 Inf. Bde.	30/07/1916	30/07/1916
Miscellaneous	Report on Fighting 53rd Machine Gun Company	30/07/1916	30/07/1916
Heading	53rd Coy M.G.C.		

Heading	War Diary For August 1916 53rd Machine Gun Company.		
War Diary	Godwaersvwelde	01/08/1916	05/08/1916
War Diary	Estaires	06/08/1916	08/08/1916
War Diary	Erquinghem	09/08/1916	12/08/1916
War Diary	Bailleul	13/08/1916	25/08/1916
War Diary	Villers Brulin	26/08/1916	31/08/1916
Heading	War Diary For September 1916 Of 53rd M.G. Company Vol 7		
Miscellaneous	From O.C. 53 M.G.C. To H.A. 53 L/Bd.	04/10/1916	04/10/1916
War Diary	Villers-Brulin	01/09/1916	09/09/1916
War Diary	Rebreuve	09/09/1916	10/09/1916
War Diary	Grouches	11/09/1916	11/09/1916
War Diary	Lealvillers	11/09/1916	17/09/1916
War Diary	Bouzincourt	18/09/1916	18/09/1916
War Diary	Forceville	19/09/1916	25/09/1916
War Diary	Authuile Wood	25/09/1916	30/09/1916
War Diary	Furceville	30/09/1916	30/09/1916
Miscellaneous	Appendix	26/09/1916	26/09/1916
Heading	War Diary For October 1916 53rd M.G. Company Vol 8		
War Diary	Authville Wood	01/10/1916	01/10/1916
War Diary	Forceville	01/10/1916	03/10/1916
War Diary	Le Meillard	04/10/1916	14/10/1916
War Diary	Albert	15/10/1916	15/10/1916
War Diary	Bailiff Wood	16/10/1916	17/10/1916
War Diary	Pozieres Cemetary	18/10/1916	23/10/1916
War Diary	Albert	24/10/1916	31/10/1916
War Diary			
Heading	War Diary For Month of November 1916 53rd M.G. Coy Vol 9		
War Diary	Pozieres	01/11/1916	05/11/1916
War Diary	Albert	05/11/1916	11/11/1916
War Diary	Pozieres	12/11/1916	14/11/1916
War Diary	Albert	14/11/1916	14/11/1916
War Diary	Pozieres & Albert	15/11/1916	19/11/1916
War Diary	Pozieres & Contay	20/11/1916	20/11/1916
War Diary	Albert & Contay	21/11/1916	21/11/1916
War Diary	Val-De-Maison	22/11/1916	23/11/1916
War Diary	Hem	24/11/1916	24/11/1916
War Diary	Grimont	25/11/1916	25/11/1916
War Diary	Coulonvillers	26/11/1916	26/11/1916
War Diary	Fontaine	27/11/1916	27/11/1916
War Diary	Lamotte Buleux	28/11/1916	30/11/1916
War Diary			
Heading	War Diary For Month Of December 1916 For 53rd Machine Gun Company. Vol 10		
War Diary	Lamotte Buleux	01/12/1916	31/12/1916
Heading	War Diary For January 1917 53rd Machine Gun Company. Vol XI		
War Diary	Drucat	01/01/1917	11/01/1917
War Diary	Beaumetz	12/01/1917	12/01/1917
War Diary	Gezaincourt	13/01/1917	14/01/1917
War Diary	Puchevillers	15/01/1917	15/01/1917
War Diary	Martinsart	16/01/1917	27/01/1917
War Diary	Mouquet Farm	28/01/1917	31/01/1917

Miscellaneous	Appendix 'A'		
Map	Grandcourt		
Heading	War Diary For 53 M.G. Coy. For February 1917 Vol 12		
War Diary	Mouquet Farm	01/02/1917	09/02/1917
War Diary	Martinsart	10/02/1917	10/02/1917
War Diary	Hedauville	11/02/1917	16/02/1917
War Diary	Zollern Trench	17/02/1917	23/02/1917
Map	Grandcourt		
Map			
Miscellaneous	Appendix A		
Map	18th Division 'B'		
Miscellaneous	Appendix B		
Heading	War Diary For March 1917 Of 53rd M.G. Coy. Vol 13		
War Diary	Mackenzie Huts (Aveluy)	01/03/1917	05/03/1917
War Diary	Petit Miraumont	06/03/1917	09/03/1917
Map			
Heading	Appendix A		
Map	18th Division "B"		
War Diary	Marlborough Huts	15/03/1917	20/03/1917
War Diary	Warloy	21/03/1917	22/03/1917
War Diary	Molliens-Au-Bois	23/03/1917	23/03/1917
War Diary	Revelles	24/03/1917	24/03/1917
War Diary	In Train	25/03/1917	26/03/1917
War Diary	Berguette	27/03/1917	31/03/1917
Heading	War Diary For 53rd Machine Gun Company April 1917 Vol 14		
War Diary	Berguette Pas-De Calais	01/04/1917	18/04/1917
War Diary	Berguette-Bethune	19/04/1917	20/04/1917
War Diary	Bethune Noeux Les Mines	21/04/1917	21/04/1917
War Diary	Noeux-Les Mines	22/04/1917	26/04/1917
War Diary	Valhuon	27/04/1917	28/04/1917
War Diary	Valhuon & Beaurains	29/04/1917	29/04/1917
War Diary	Beaurains	30/04/1917	30/04/1917
Heading	War Diary for May 1917 53 M.G. Company Vol 15		
War Diary	Beaurains	01/05/1917	01/05/1917
War Diary	Neuville Vitasse	02/05/1917	04/05/1917
War Diary	N.22.d	05/05/1917	06/05/1917
War Diary	N.30.c.34	07/05/1917	11/05/1917
War Diary	T.5b.7.8	11/05/1917	21/05/1917
War Diary	S.17.	22/05/1917	31/05/1917
Map	Map 'A'		
Heading	Map 'A' Appendix to War Diary May 1917 53 M.G. Coy.		
Map	Map 'B'		
Heading	Map B Appendix to War Diary May 1917 53 M.G. Coy.		
War Diary	S 17 Central	01/06/1917	02/06/1917
War Diary	M 366	03/06/1917	09/06/1917
Map	Map 'A'		
Heading	Map 'A' Appendix to War Diary May 1917 53 M.G. Coy		
Map	Map 'B'		
Heading	Map B Appendix to War Diary May 1917 53 M.G. Coy.		
War Diary	Souastre	19/06/1917	03/07/1917
War Diary	Steenvorde Area	04/07/1917	31/07/1917

Miscellaneous	Ypres Operations	03/07/1917	03/07/1917
Miscellaneous	Battalion Headquarters		
Miscellaneous	A Company		
Miscellaneous	B Company		
Miscellaneous	C Company.		
Miscellaneous	D Company.		
Miscellaneous	Half Section 53rd. Machine Gun Company.		
Miscellaneous	The Following Messages Were Sent to Brigade Headquarters.		
Miscellaneous	General Remarks		
Miscellaneous	Du.		
Miscellaneous	When marking up documents for copying please tick the appropriate box.		
Miscellaneous	Ypres Operation	03/07/1917	03/07/1917
Miscellaneous	Battalion Headquarters		
Miscellaneous	A Company		
Miscellaneous	B Company		
Miscellaneous	C Company.		
Miscellaneous	D Company.		
Miscellaneous	Half Section 53rd. Machine Gun Company.		
Miscellaneous	The Following Messages Were Sent to Brigade Headquarters.		
Miscellaneous	General Remarks		
Miscellaneous	Appendix "A"		
Miscellaneous	Appendix D		
Miscellaneous	53rd Machine Gun Company.	25/07/1917	25/07/1917
Miscellaneous	Appendix X		
Miscellaneous	Ypres Operations		
War Diary	Ypres Operations	01/08/1917	31/08/1917
Diagram etc	Identification Trace for use with Artillery Maps.		
Map	Identification Trace for use with Artillery Maps.		
Heading	53rd Coy Machine Gun Corps War Diary for September 1917 Vol 19		
War Diary	Rubrouck Area	01/09/1917	30/09/1917
Heading	53 Machine Gun Coy War Diary for October 1917 Vol 20		
War Diary	St. Janter Biezen	01/10/1917	08/10/1917
War Diary	Ypres Operations.	09/10/1917	19/10/1917
War Diary	Poelcappelle	20/10/1917	22/10/1917
War Diary	Ypres Operations Poelcappelle	22/10/1917	30/10/1917
War Diary	Pegwell Camp Proven	01/11/1917	30/11/1917
War Diary	Signal Fm	01/12/1917	05/12/1917
War Diary	Box Camp. A 5c 19	06/12/1917	10/12/1917
War Diary	Marguerite Camp	11/12/1917	17/12/1917
War Diary	Herzeele	18/12/1917	27/12/1917
War Diary	Proven	28/12/1917	28/12/1917
War Diary	Marguerite Camp	29/12/1917	31/12/1917

W02040|3

18TH DIVISION

53RD MACH. GUN COY.

FEB 1916-DEC 1917

53 M G Coy

Vol 1

War Diary.

53rd Machine Gun Company.

Feb 9th - Feb 28th

Dec 17

March 1 - March 31st

1916

Instructions regarding War Diaries and Intelligence Summaries are contained in F. S. Regs., Part II. and the Staff Manual respectively. Title Pages will be prepared in manuscript.

WAR DIARY
or
~~INTELLIGENCE SUMMARY~~
(Erase heading not required.)

Army Form C. 2118

Place	Date	Hour	Summary of Events and Information	Remarks and references to Appendices
Havre	9 Feb	4 am 2 PM	Unit arrived in Havre roadstead. On board SS Courfield(?) with Transport of 44. 46. 51. 53. 53. 58 Coys. Personnel of these Coys on S.S. Lydia. Composition of Coy as per Appendix (1). Landed at 2 PM to Docks Rest Camp. 1 G.S. Waggon A.S.C. driver and 2 H D horses joined unit	
"	10 "	"	Completing establishment of equipment. Casualty one man admitted to hospital	
"	11	"	Orders received to proceed to join 18 Division	
"	12 "	"	Parade 7 am Entrained at Point 3 Havre at 8 Train left 10.39 Halt at	
		8.45	Montrolier(?) Buchy(?) Arrived Mericourt(?) 8.45.	
ALBERT	13 "	2 am	Arrived ALBERT 2 am. billetted in RUE BECOURT. Unit attached to 53 Brigade Brigadier General MACANDREW.	
"	14	"	Inspected line held by Brigade Sections E2 & E3. now held by 10 Royal Berks and 8 Norfolks	
"	15	—	Surveyed defences of Albert. No 1 Section working on UZNA redoubt(?) No 2(?) Section working on TARA redoubt	
"	16	— 5 pm	Weather wet. Took Section Commanders over E2 & E3. Artillery of 32 Division on left of 18 Division shelled AVELERS(?) [illegible]	

Instructions regarding War Diaries and Intelligence Summaries are contained in F. S. Regs., Part II. and the Staff Manual respectively. Title Pages will be prepared in manuscript.

WAR DIARY
or
INTELLIGENCE SUMMARY
(Erase heading not required.)

Army Form C. 2118

Place	Date	Hour	Summary of Events and Information	Remarks and references to Appendices
ALBERT.	17.2.16	—	In touch with 55 M.G. Coy. (Capt HEYLAND) on right (Holding E1)	
– " –	18.2.16	—	No 1 Gun No 1 Section (Sgt TOZER) moved into trench 127 just N of sector E1.	
		6 P.M.	Section at BUIRE on Flank O	
– " –	19.2.16		Instructed to have 4 guns in each Sector as soon as possible	
– " –	20.2.16	10 A.M.	2 Guns No 4 Section 2/Lt POCOCK into E2 Sector	
		5 P.M.	Remaining 3 Guns No 1 Section Lt FALKNER and 2/Lt PARSONS moved into E3 moving delayed by the shelling of Sector HQ	
– " –	21.2.16	—	E2 One Gun in ARBROATH St One in DUNDEE St E3 One Gun DALHOUSIE One BRAY St One 127	
		7 P.M.	3rd Gun No 4 Section moved into E2	
– " –	2			
– " –	22.2.16	—	Quiet on Sector front.	
		6 P.M.	Enemy attacked TAMBOUR on right. Reserve section stood to unnecessarily	
– " –	23.2.16	10.30	Manned Redoubts UZNA and TARA 2 Guns each	
		2.30	Defences of ALBERT manned for inspection by Divisional Commander	

1875 Wt. W593/826 1,000,000 4/15 J.B.C. & A. A.D.S.S./Forms/C. 2118.

Army Form C. 2118

Instructions regarding War Diaries and Intelligence Summaries are contained in F. S. Regs., Part II. and the Staff Manual respectively. Title Pages will be prepared in manuscript.

WAR DIARY
or
INTELLIGENCE SUMMARY
(Erase heading not required.)

Place	Date	Hour	Summary of Events and Information	Remarks and references to Appendices
ALBERT	23/2/16	3 P.M.	No 3 Section relieved No 1 in E3.	
		7 P.M.	No 2 Section (2Lt GILBEY) relieved No 4 Section in E2	
			E2. Guns in trenches 113. 115. KINGSGATE ST & ARBROATH	
			Very Cold. with Snow	
— " —	24/2/16	3 P.M.	Connected Section Commanders Dug Out E3 with Sector Switchboard	
			Hard Frost. Guns being fired intermittently	
— " —	25/2/16	10.30	Inspection of Transport Nos 1 & 4 Sections & details by Brigadier	
		2.	Carrying party No 1 Section materials to E2.	
			Snow Hard Frost	
— " —	26/2/16	—	Situation Quiet Work impossible on account of Snow	
			Slight Thaw	
— " —	27/2/16	—	Situation Normal E2. Intermittent firing	
			E3. Tunnel emplacement DALHOUSIE ST taken over from Lewis Gun	
			New emplacement started in DALHOUSIE ST	

1875 Wt. W593/826 1,000,000 4/15 J.B.C. & A. A.D.S.S./Forms/C. 2118.

Instructions regarding War Diaries and Intelligence Summaries are contained in F. S. Regs., Part II. and the Staff Manual respectively. Title Pages will be prepared in manuscript.

WAR DIARY
or
~~INTELLIGENCE SUMMARY~~
(Erase heading not required.)

Army Form C. 2118

Place	Date	Hour	Summary of Events and Information	Remarks and references to Appendices
ALBERT	28-2-16		E 2. Situation Quiet. 11.20 p.m. enemy fired on M.G. near 115. Position not located	
			E 3 Normal.	
"	29-2-16		E 2. Situation Normal Enemy M.G. Active	
			E 3 Situation Normal	
			Orders issued for relief by 14 Bde M.G. Coy (~~Appendix B~~)	~~B~~
~~1-3-16~~			~~E 2 Situation Quiet. Sentry reports flash of M.G. No. 4 of 115~~ ~~10 Ltking [illegible] dropped near 115~~	
			~~E 3 Situation Normal~~	~~C~~
			~~Brigade H.Q. moved to La Houssoye. (Appendix C)~~	

1875 Wt. W593/826 1,000,000 4/15 J.B.C. & A. A.D.S.S./Forms/C. 2118.

Instructions regarding War Diaries and Intelligence Summaries are contained in F. S. Regs., Part II. and the Staff Manual respectively. Title Pages will be prepared in manuscript.

WAR DIARY
or
INTELLIGENCE SUMMARY
(Erase heading not required.)

Army Form C. 2118

Place	Date	Hour	Summary of Events and Information	Remarks and references to Appendices
Albert	1/3/16	—	E3 Situation quiet	
			E2 Situation quiet. Enemy's M.G. N of E of trench 115 active. 10 light shells dropped near 115	
		7 PM	18 Division relieved by 14 Inf. Bde. 19 Lancashire Fusiliers in E2. 2 Manchesters in E3 (vide 53 R/Bde orders BM 342)	
			Bde Report Centre opened at LAHOUSSOYE. 18 Division transferred to 13 CORPS (53 R/Bde BM 345)	
— " —	2/3/16		53 Bde M.G. Coy. relieved by two sections 14 Bde M.G. (two 2 guns in E1) Relief commenced 11.30 am. No 3 Section returned 2.30 pm No 2 at 4.45	
		3 PM	Headquarters handed over at 3 pm. Proceeded by sections to FRANVILLERS. First section left ALBERT 3 pm last 6 pm. Billets in FRANVILLERS on C road	
FRANVILLERS	3/3/16		Resting in Billets. Other battalions in FRANVILLERS 10 ESSEX. 8 Suffolks	
—	4/3/16		Resting in Billets. Bad weather	
— " —	5/3/16		Resting in Billets. Staff Ride over training area.	
— " —	6/3/16		Resting in Billets Training recommenced.	
—	7/3/16		Resting in Billets. Instructional class formed of eight men from each of NORFOLK. SUFFOLK & ESSEX Regts	[signature]

1875 Wt. W593/826 1,000,000 4/15 J.B.C. & A. A.D.S.S./Forms/C. 2118.

Instructions regarding War Diaries and Intelligence Summaries are contained in F. S. Regs., Part II. and the Staff Manual respectively. Title Pages will be prepared in manuscript.

Army Form C. 2118

WAR DIARY
or
INTELLIGENCE SUMMARY
(Erase heading not required.)

Place	Date	Hour	Summary of Events and Information	Remarks and references to Appendices
FRANVILLERS	8/3/16	–	Resting in Billets	
— . —	9/3/16	–	OC Coy with acting Brigadier (Colonel Dowell Royal Berkshire Regt) Brigade Major and Bde Signal Officer to BRAY to go over sectors Z1 & Z2 (MARICOURT) held by 89 Bde 30 Division.	
— . —	10/3/16	–	Training in Billets	
— . —	11/3/16	–	Training in Billets 2/Lt Tulloch 2/Lt GILBERT to BRAY to view trenches	
— . —	12/3/16	–	Training in Billets CAPT DUNLOP and Lt FALKNER to BRAY to view trenches	
— . —	13/3/16	–	Preparing for move.	
— . —	14/3/16	10 AM	Company left FRANVILLERS 10 AM and proceeded via RIBEMONT and MORLANCOURT to ETINHAM. Arrived 4 pm occupied in conjunction with 10 Bn ESSEX Regt ETINHAM CAMP. Bombs dropped near camp from enemy aeroplane about 10 pm.	
ETINHAM	15/3/16	9 AM	Company moved by sections ETINHAM to BRAY. Headquarters RUE DU PORT established 9 AM	
·		5 PM	Sections 1. 3 & 4 moved to trenches. No 1 relieved M.M.G. (2nd) in Z2 subsector No 4 M.M.G. battery guns (2 guns) in Z1. No 3 Lewis Guns in MARICOURT Defences	[initials]

1875 Wt. W593/826 1,000,000 4/15 J.B.C. & A. A.D.S.S./Forms/C. 2118.

Instructions regarding War Diaries and Intelligence Summaries are contained in F. S. Regs., Part II. and the Staff Manual respectively. Title Pages will be prepared in manuscript.

WAR DIARY
or
INTELLIGENCE SUMMARY
(Erase heading not required.)

Army Form C. 2118

Place	Date	Hour	Summary of Events and Information	Remarks and references to Appendices
~~16-3-16~~ BRAY	16/3/16		Guns in Z1 Trenches 21 & 27. Z2 28 support & 31 Support – MARICOURT Defences. PERONNE RD barrier. MOUND KEEP. WEST KEEP. SUFFOLKS in Z1 ESSEXS into ~~[illegible]~~ Z2 at 9 P.M relieving KINGS LIVERPOOLS NORFOLKS in MARICOURT	
~~17-3-16~~ — " —	17/3/16	9.35	Z1. Quiet. 3946 Pte Harris seriously wounded at 9.35 a.m. rifle or machine gun died at CORBIE same evening Z2 Quiet	
~~18-3-16~~ — " —	18/3/16		Z1 } Z2 } Nothing to report	
~~19-3-16~~	19/3/16	2 PM	No 2 Section to Z1. No 4 Section to MARICOURT defences. No 3 Section to Z2 No 1 Section Rest. Situation Quiet. Work on H.Q dugout in PRIVET AVENUE Commenced.	
~~20-3-16~~	20/3/16		No 6372 Pte Stainton E.T. No 6347 Pte Lewis M.H. wounded by shell fire Situation Quiet. Platform put in by 31 support	[signature]

1875 Wt. W593/826 1,000,000 4/15 J.B.C. & A. A.D.S.S./Forms/C. 2118.

Instructions regarding War Diaries and Intelligence Summaries are contained in F. S. Regs., Part II. and the Staff Manual respectively. Title Pages will be prepared in manuscript.

WAR DIARY
or
INTELLIGENCE SUMMARY
(Erase heading not required.)

Army Form C. 2118

Place	Date	Hour	Summary of Events and Information	Remarks and references to Appendices
BRAY	21/3/16		Quiet in both sectors FRENCH emplacement in 22 trench cleared & repairs commenced	
— " —	22/3/16		Nothing to report	
— " —	23/3/16		No 4 section to Z1. No 2 section to MARICOURT. No 1 section (2/Lt DAVIDSON) to Z2 No 3 section to rest. Position in MACHINE GUN WOOD occupied. Lt FALKINER to hospital sick	
— " —	24/3/16		Z1 Quiet Z2. Quiet H.Q. ~~[illegible]~~ section moved to dug out by support line end of Castle Avenue	
— " —	25/3/16		Z1 Normal bearings taken for indirect fire Z2. M.G. WOOD Dug out strengthened	[initials]

1875 Wt. W593/826 1,000,000 4/15 J.B.C. & A. A.D.S.S./Forms/C. 2118.

Army Form C. 2118

Instructions regarding War Diaries and Intelligence Summaries are contained in F. S. Regs., Part II. and the Staff Manual respectively. Title Pages will be prepared in manuscript.

WAR DIARY
or
INTELLIGENCE SUMMARY
(Erase heading not required.)

Place	Date	Hour	Summary of Events and Information	Remarks and references to Appendices
BRAY	26/3/16		Z1. Normal. Gun fired at night: on (1) HARDECOURT traversing from CHURCH to S end of village. (2) NAMELESS WOOD and enemy's tracks expenditure 500 rounds. Z2. HAYSTACKS emplacement building.	
— " —	27/3/16		Z1. Normal Gun fired on NAMELESS WOOD. SUPPORT COPSE. BOIS d'en HAUT Z2. HAYSTACKS platform finished No 2 Section to Z1. No 4 section to REST No 3 to Z2 No 1 to Maricourt defences.	
— " —	28/3/16		Z1 Normal "FOREST" emplacement begun. Z2. Normal work on HAYSTACKS dug out	
— " —	29/3/16		Nothing to report. Lt FALKNER returns to duty	
— " —				

[signature]

1875 Wt. W593/826 1,000,000 4/15 J.B.C. & A. A.D.S.S./Forms/C. 2118.

Instructions regarding War Diaries and Intelligence Summaries are contained in F. S. Regs., Part II. and the Staff Manual respectively. Title Pages will be prepared in manuscript.

WAR DIARY
or
INTELLIGENCE SUMMARY

(Erase heading not required.)

Army Form C. 2118

Place	Date	Hour	Summary of Events and Information	Remarks and references to Appendices
BRAY	30/3/16		Z1 Normal. "FRENCH" position occupied work started on dug out at FOREST gun. 'SAP' gun handed to Z2 Z2 Gun moved to SAP.	
— " —	31/3/16.		Z1. Work on FOREST gun position Z2. Dugout at HAYSTACKS. Ammunition expended 400 rounds	

1875 Wt. W593/826 1,000,000 4/15 J.B.C. & A. A.D.S.S./Forms/C. 2118.

XVIII

53 M G Coy
Vol 2

War Diary

53rd Coy Machine Gun Corps.

April 1916.

Army Form C. 2118.

Instructions regarding War Diaries and Intelligence Summaries are contained in F. S. Regs., Part II. and the Staff Manual respectively. Title Pages will be prepared in manuscript.

WAR DIARY
or
INTELLIGENCE SUMMARY

(Erase heading not required.)

Place	Date	Hour	Summary of Events and Information	Remarks and references to Appendices
BRAY	1/4/16	–	Z1 Situation Quiet. Officers dug out and "FOREST" emplacement continued.	
			Z2 Situation Quiet Haystack emplacement continued.	
			No 4 Section in Z1. No 2 section resting in BRAY. No 1 Section Z2.	
			No 3 Section MARICOURT DEFENCES.	
	2/4/16	–	Z1 Quiet. I 'FOREST' emplacement continued. Platform in "FRENCH" emplacement raised to give better field of fire	
			Z2. Quiet. HAYSTACKS dugout continued	
	3/4/16	–	Z1. Quiet. 1. 'DUMP' emplacement commenced. 'FOREST' emplacement finished and dug out commenced.	
			In conjunction with No 3 Section fired on NAMELESS WOOD Bois d'en HAUT. 'CLAPHAM FARM' SUPPORT COPSE tracks leading from wood were searched. Firing between	
		4–5 a.m.	4 & 5 am 1500 rounds	
			Z2. Situation Quiet	
	4/4/16	–	Z1 Quiet. DUMP & FOREST position improved	
			Z2 Quiet Two new dug outs commenced.	

2449 Wt. W14957/M90 750,000 1/16 J.B.C. & A. Forms/C.2118/12.

Instructions regarding War Diaries and Intelligence Summaries are contained in F. S. Regs., Part II. and the Staff Manual respectively. Title Pages will be prepared in manuscript.

WAR DIARY
or
INTELLIGENCE SUMMARY
(Erase heading not required.)

Army Form C. 2118.

Place	Date	Hour	Summary of Events and Information	Remarks and references to Appendices
BRAY	5/4/16	–	No 3 Section to Z2. No 2 to Z1. No 4 to MARICOURT. No 1 to BRAY. Z1. Situation Quiet. DUMP & FOREST work carried on. Z2 Quiet. No wood available to continue work. Inspected by R.E. & instructions given "HAYSTACKS" gun in position.	
– " –	6/4/16		Z1 Quiet. Work as above continued. between 3 am & 4.15 am fired with 2 guns (conjunction with No 4) into NAMELESS WOOD BOIS d'la HAUT. SUPPORT COPSE. Guns in splendid condition Enemy M.G. opened on us at 4 a.m. shots waist high. Expenditure 2,500 rounds. Z2. New dug out for HAYSTACKS commenced.	
– " –	7/4/16	–	Z1. Quiet. Work as above carried on. 1 Gun No 2 & 1 No 4 searched MONTAUBAN and communication trenches	
		9–11 pm	running from "A" Expenditure 3000 rounds.	
			Z2. Quiet. HAYSTACKS & M.G. WOOD dug out continued.	
– " –	8/4/16	–	Z1 Quiet work as before. No firing. Z2. Quiet. Work as before. Range cards completed for all positions	
– " –	9/4/16		Z1 Quiet work as before Z2. – " – – " – No 3 Gun movement [illegible] during dark in LITTLE WYREST	

2449 Wt. W14957/M90 750,000 1/16 J.B.C. & A. Forms/C.2118/12.

Army Form C. 2118.

Instructions regarding War Diaries and Intelligence Summaries are contained in F. S. Regs., Part II. and the Staff Manual respectively. Title Pages will be prepared in manuscript.

WAR DIARY
or
INTELLIGENCE SUMMARY
(Erase heading not required.)

Place	Date	Hour	Summary of Events and Information	Remarks and references to Appendices
~~10/4/1~~ BRAY	10/4/16	-	Z1. Quiet work as before. Z2 -"- -"-	
-"-	11/4/16	-	No1 Section to Z2. No 2 to MARICOURT. No 4 to ~~BRAY~~ Z1 No 3 to BRAY. Z1. Quiet. Work carried on and working party to WEST KEEP. Z.2 Quiet Nothing to report	
	12/4/16	-	Z1 Quiet. FOREST dug out timbered. Reserve SAA stored in recess in BAROSSA Avenue. Z2. Quiet Nothing to report. 2/Lt Gilby returns to duty ex hospital	
	13/4/16	-	Z1. Enemy's artillery active between ~~2~~ & 4 am. Work continued. Z2. Nothing to report.	
	14/4/16		Z1. Quiet work on "DUMP" continued. Z2 Nothing to report. Section of 89 M.G. Coy under instruction withdrawn and returned to rest	

2449 Wt. W14957/M90 750,000 1/16 J.B.C. & A. Forms/C.2118/12.

Instructions regarding War Diaries and Intelligence Summaries are contained in F. S. Regs., Part II. and the Staff Manual respectively. Title Pages will be prepared in manuscript.

WAR DIARY
or
INTELLIGENCE SUMMARY
(Erase heading not required.)

Army Form C. 2118.

Place	Date	Hour	Summary of Events and Information	Remarks and references to Appendices
BRAY.	15/4/16	–	Z1 Quiet. FOREST emplacement occupied. No 2 Section supplying party for "dump".	
			Z2. Nothing to report.	
	16/4/16		Z1/Z2 Nothing to report. 2/Lt Tulloch to duty from Divisional school. 2/Lt Townsend to Divisional school.	
	17/4/16	–	~~Z1. Quiet.~~ No 3 Section to Z2. No 1 to MARICOURT. No 2 to Z1. No 4 Section to BRAY	
	17/4/16		Z1 "DUMP" emplacement occupied. Alternative to FRENCH emplacement finished & to be occasionally occupied. Z2. Clearing trenches near emplacements.	
	18/4/16.		Z1 Quiet. Z2 Sappers arrived to work on ~~emplacement~~ dugout carried on.	
	19/4/16		Z1. Evening heavy shelling of left of this sector. SAP gun shelled with shrapnel. No attempt on part of enemy to leave trenches. M'Guns did not open. Pte TOULSON wounded shrapnel.	

2449 Wt. W14957/M90 750,000 1/16 J.B.C. & A. Forms/C.2118/12.

Army Form C. 2118.

Instructions regarding War Diaries and Intelligence Summaries are contained in F. S. Regs., Part II. and the Staff Manual respectively. Title Pages will be prepared in manuscript.

WAR DIARY
or
INTELLIGENCE SUMMARY

(Erase heading not required.)

Place	Date	Hour	Summary of Events and Information	Remarks and references to Appendices
19/4/16 sector BRAY	Bt 19/4/16 cont.	–	Z 2. Heavy bombardment on left (Z 1) and on right of this sector. 568 Rounds fired along enemy wire.	
– " –	20/4/16	–	Z 1 Normal. Timbering on "DUMP" dugout, and new entrance to "FOREST" dugout. Z 2 Normal. Work on WYREST dugout.	
– " –	21/4/16	–	Z 1 } Z 2 } Normal. Work continued as above.	
– " –	22/4/16		– No 4 Section to Z 1. – No 2 Section to BRAY – No 1 to Z 2 No 3 to MARICOURT Z 1. Post sited as alternative to "SHP". Gun on left of Y 3 covering right of Z 1 is A 23 c 53.70. Z 2 Normal	
– " –	23/4/16		Z 1 } Z 2 } Normal. 6179 Pte Moses, P. wounded in head 8.30 P.M.	
– " –	24/4/16		Z 1 } Z 2 } Normal work carried on as above.	

2449 Wt. W14957/M90 750,000 1/16 J.B.C. & A. Forms/C.2118/12.

Army Form C. 2118.

WAR DIARY
or
INTELLIGENCE SUMMARY

(Erase heading not required.)

Instructions regarding War Diaries and Intelligence Summaries are contained in F. S. Regs., Part II. and the Staff Manual respectively. Title Pages will be prepared in manuscript.

Place	Date	Hour	Summary of Events and Information	Remarks and references to Appendices
~~25/4/16~~ BRAY	25/4/16	–	Z1. New emplacement started as alternative to SAP Aiming Posts put out for FOREST gun. Z2. Normal Bell heard 12.30 - 12.45 a.m. from direction MAUREPAS	
– " –	26/4/16	–	Z1 Normal. 250 rounds fired at working party at R17 a 75 82 at 9.30 p.m. by SAP gun. Alternative emplacement to SAP finished Z2 11.30 PM. SOS A2 sent 750 rounds fired from Little Wyre St Gun along Enemy's [illegible]	
– " –	27/4/16	–	Z1 Normal Z2. 1.30 a.m. Raid carried out by 54 Bde on left. Little Wyre St gun cooperated. Stoppage due to broken muzzle grip Rectified	
– " –	28/4/16	–	Z1 Enemy shelled LOWESTOFT Street 9.30 p.m. SAP Gun opened. Z2 Normal	
– " –	29/4/16	–	Z1 } Z2 } Normal preparing for relief	

2449 Wt. W14957/M90 750,000 1/16 J.B.C. & A. Forms/C.2118/12.

Instructions regarding War Diaries and Intelligence Summaries are contained in F. S. Regs., Part II. and the Staff Manual respectively. Title Pages will be prepared in manuscript.

WAR DIARY
or
INTELLIGENCE SUMMARY

(Erase heading not required.)

Army Form C. 2118.

Place	Date	Hour	Summary of Events and Information	Remarks and references to Appendices
BRAY	30/4/16		Company relieved by 89 M.G. Coy Capt Roxburgh No2 Section advance party to SAILLY LORETTE. 8 AM Sections at MARICOURT & trenches relieved during the day Relief complete 2.30pm All sections in SAILLY LORETTE 7.30pm	
Map Positions of Guns	April 1916		Ref. Trench Map 1/10000 MARICOURT	
			Z1 { DUMP – A 23a 23.52	
			FRENCH – " 60.94	
			HALLS HILL (SPION KOP) – " 62.69	
			SAP – A 16b 80.82	
			FOREST – A 17c 18.30	
			Z2 { HAYSTACKS – A 16a 41.52	
			LITTLE WYREST – " 10.52	
			M.G. WOOD (2 guns) – A 15b 88.48	

John K. Roxburgh Capt
5-5-16

FROM. O.C. 53rd M.G. Coy

To D.A.G. 3rd Echelon.

Herewith War Diary for month of ~~April~~ May of unit under my command.

John L. Dunlop

Major

M.G.C 178.
2-6-16.

53 M.G. Coy
Vol 3

XVIII

War Diary for month of May 1916.

53rd Company

Machine Gun Corps.

[illegible signature]
Major.

Instructions regarding War Diaries and Intelligence Summaries are contained in F. S. Regs., Part II. and the Staff Manual respectively. Title Pages will be prepared in manuscript.

WAR DIARY
or
~~INTELLIGENCE SUMMARY~~
(Erase heading not required.)

Army Form C. 2118

Place	Date	Hour	Summary of Events and Information	Remarks and references to Appendices
SAILLY LAURETTE	1/5/16	8.15 am	Company moved from SAILLY LAURETTE to DAOURS. via CORBIE & AUBIGNY long halt at AUBIGNY. arrived 1.10. Very hot. Men & mules travelled very well. Very hot day.	
DAOURS	2/5/16	5 am	Company moved to LONGPRE by AMIENS. Billeting party (O.C. CSM & cyclist) left at 4.45. Company arrived 10.30 am, in very good condition. [illegible]	
LONGPRE	3/5/16	—	Sections under section officers unpacking limbers	
— " —	4/5/16	—	Company parades. Gun drill, manual, lectures	
AILLY sur SOMME	5/5/16	—	Company moves to AILLY sur SOMME. O.C. & transport at 11. Remainder at 3. Leave commences	
— " —	6/5/16	—	Overhauled limbers, painted guns. squad & [illegible] drill	
— " —	7/5/16	—	Inspections for Ration kit clothing equipment etc	
— " —	8/5/16	—	Gun drill 9-12. 12 to 1 Squad & Rifle	
— " —	9/5/16	—	Route march. 2/Lt Townsend from Div. School. 2/Lt GILBERT to Div School	

1875 Wt. W593/826 1,000,000 4/15 J.B.C. & A. A.D.S.S./Forms/C. 2118.

Instructions regarding War Diaries and Intelligence Summaries are contained in F. S. Regs., Part II. and the Staff Manual respectively. Title Pages will be prepared in manuscript.

WAR DIARY
or
~~INTELLIGENCE SUMMARY~~
(Erase heading not required.)

Army Form C. 2118

Place	Date	Hour	Summary of Events and Information	Remarks and references to Appendices
RILLY-SUR-SOMME	10/5/16	—	Section drill 9-12 noon. 12 noon-1 pm Company drill. Leave party Capt T.K. Dunlop Sgt [illegible] L/Cpl Trussler.	
— " —	11/5/16	—	Overhauling limbers & unpacking all HQ. stores packed.	
— " —	12/5/16	—	No 1 Section 2 fighting limbers, & 1 SAA limber & 2 pack mules. tactical handling No 3 Section stoppages Gas Helmets [illegible] rounds on range. 2 & 4 Gun Drill	
— " —	13/5/16	—	1.2.& 4 tactical handling. No 3 on range. 12-1 Company parade with C.S.M.	
— " —	14/5/16	—	Church parade.	
— " —	15/5/16	—	Physical training. Explanation of Dial Sights. No 1 Section stoppages with Gas Helmets	
— " —	16/5/16		Tactical handling at POULAINVILLE by 2.3.&4. No 1 on range.	
— " —	17/5/16		1-3 Section tactical handling at POULAINVILLE	
— " —	18/5/16		1.2.3 Section tactical handling at POULAINVILLE. 4 Section on range.	
— " —	19/5/16		Company Parade for tactical training.	

1875 Wt. W593/826 1,000,000 4/15 J.B.C. & A. A.D.S.S./Forms/C. 2118.

Instructions regarding War Diaries and Intelligence Summaries are contained in F. S. Regs., Part II. and the Staff Manual respectively. Title Pages will be prepared in manuscript.

WAR DIARY
or
~~INTELLIGENCE~~ SUMMARY
(Erase heading not required.)

Army Form C. 2118

Place	Date	Hour	Summary of Events and Information	Remarks and references to Appendices
RILLY sur SOMME	20/5/16	6.45 am	Company Parade with Bde for battle training on POULAINVILLE trenches.	
—"—	21/5/16	—	Church Services	
—"—	22/5/16	—	Company parade 9 am packing limbers & equipment.	
—"—	23/5/16	7 am	Company moved RILLY sur SOMME to CORBIE. Long halt half way between AMIENS & DAOURS. Company arrived 4.30	
CORBIE	24/5/16	3 pm	Company moved CORBIE to BRAY. bad weather company arrived 8.45 pm	
BRAY	25/5/16	—	Nos 2 3 & 4 sections to trenches. O.C.'s section & three per section left at 1. No 3 section (2 guns) left at 1. Remainder at 8. Took over 2 gun positions from 91st M.G. Coy 10 gun positions from 21st M.G. Coy. Wet night relief difficult completed by 12.30 am 26	
—"—	26/5/16	—	No report from sections	
—"—	27/5/16	—	Nothing to report.	

1875 Wt. W593/826 1,000,000 4/15 J.B.C. & A. A.D.S.S./Forms/C. 2118.

Instructions regarding War Diaries and Intelligence Summaries are contained in F. S. Regs., Part II. and the Staff Manual respectively. Title Pages will be prepared in manuscript.

WAR DIARY
or
~~INTELLIGENCE SUMMARY~~
(Erase heading not required.)

Army Form C. 2118

Place	Date	Hour	Summary of Events and Information	Remarks and references to Appendices
BRAY	28/5/16	—	No 2 Section No 1 gun position strengthened.	
	29/5/16	—	No 2 Section to CARNOY. No 4 to A1 No 1 to A.2. No 3 to BRAY relief completed 7 P.M. No 7 gun traversed by M.G. fire during night. Casualty 4927 Pte Jones (shell shock).	
	30/5/16	1230	a.m. and after No 1 gun traversed enemy's parapet at intervals expenditure 250 rounds	
	31/5/16		A1 Work on mine dugout at No 4 gun & strutting of gallery continued A2 Deepening, narrowing & strengthening of entrance to Central Depot ([illegible]) Enemy's M.G. played on Glasgow Street during night.	

[illegible signature]
Major

1875 Wt. W593/826 1,000,000 4/15 J.B.C. & A. A.D.S.S./Forms/C. 2118.

FROM OC 53 M.G. Coy

TO D A G 3 Echelon

Herewith WAR DIARY for above mentioned unit for month of June 1916 War diary for July is being sent via 18 Division

M.G.C. 336.
6-8-16

[signature]
Major

18 JUNE

53 MGC

Vol 4

War Diary

June 1916

53rd Machine Gun Company

Instructions regarding War Diaries and Intelligence Summaries are contained in F. S. Regs., Part II. and the Staff Manual respectively. Title Pages will be prepared in manuscript.

WAR DIARY
or
INTELLIGENCE SUMMARY
(Erase heading not required.)

Army Form C. 2118

Place	Date	Hour	Summary of Events and Information	Remarks and references to Appendices
Bray	1/6/16		Sector A1. Situation quiet. Work continued on Dump gun emplacement. No 1 gun fired on enemy wiring party. S.A.A. expended 250 rounds.	
			Sector A2 Situation quiet. Work continued on Central Depot. Three trench mortar shells fell on bay near No 7 gun but did no damage. They fell about 9 pm on night 31st.	
	2/6/16		" A2. There was a battle this evening during which Nos 5 & 6 guns traversed the enemy parapet. Nos 7 & 8 guns did not fire as they were too near the enemy. Certain amount of shelling around Nos 5 & 6 guns during the battle. Work done – Entrance to Central Depot, traverse & dug out to No 5 gun strengthened. S.A.A. expended 3000 rounds.	
			A1 Nothing to Report on this sector.	
	3/6/16		A1 Situation quiet. Dug out at [illegible] guns being continued. A shelter being made at No 1 gun. During the previous night's bombardment Nos 1 & 2 guns fired a belt each into the enemy parapet. Work done – all belts filled. Drawing S.A.A. from Carnoy reserve. S.A.A. expended 400 rounds.	

1875 Wt. W593/826 1,000,000 4/15 J.B.C. & A. A.D.S.S./Forms/C. 2118.

Army Form C. 2118

Instructions regarding War Diaries and Intelligence Summaries are contained in F. S. Regs., Part II. and the Staff Manual respectively. Title Pages will be prepared in manuscript.

WAR DIARY
or
INTELLIGENCE SUMMARY
(Erase heading not required.)

Place	Date	Hour	Summary of Events and Information	Remarks and references to Appendices
Bray	3/6/16		Section A2. Situation quiet. Narrowing entrance to Central Depot & making S.A.A. recesses. Traverse & dug out at No 5 gun strengthened. The guns which fired last night ran very well only one or two simple stoppages occurring.	
"	4/6/16		" A1 Situation normal. Gun teams at No 1 & No 2 emplacements relieved by men of No 4 section from 10 am to 9 pm	
"			" A2 Nothing to report on this sector.	
"	5/6/16		" A1 Situation quiet. Enemy M.G's less active. Dug out at No 3 gun nearing completion.	
			" A2 During a bombardment some way on left No 5 gun fired intermittent bursts at enemy parapet between 10 pm & midnight. One or two rifle grenades fell near No 5 gun during day & a mortar fell near Sp[?] shelter at No 8 gun.	
"	6/6/16		" A1 Situation quiet - Nothing to report	
			A2 More enemy activity than on previous nights.	
"	7/6/16		" A1 Several rifle grenades sent over by the Boche. Lewis gun fired on craters at intervals during night.	
			" A2 Situation normal - Work continued on Central Depot	
"	8/6/16		" A1 Situation normal - Strengthening dug outs & emplacements.	
			A2 Enemy shelled front line & counter attack line & Peronne Rd. Central Depot work continued.	

1875 Wt. W593/826 1,000,000 4/15 J.B.C. & A. A.D.S.S./Forms/C. 2118.

Instructions regarding War Diaries and Intelligence Summaries are contained in F. S. Regs., Part II. and the Staff Manual respectively. Title Pages will be prepared in manuscript.

Army Form C. 2118

WAR DIARY
or
INTELLIGENCE SUMMARY
(Erase heading not required.)

Place	Date	Hour	Summary of Events and Information	Remarks and references to Appendices
Bray	9/6/16		Section A.1. Enemy battery appeared to be registering this sector. Lewis guns fired on working party. Work on battle emplacements continued.	
"			A 2. Enemy T Mortars active during day break. – appeared to be registering our front line. S.A.A. being carried to Central Depot.	
"	10/6/16		A 1. Enemy shelled our trench at L/C Rose gun. L/C Rose and Pte Burroughs killed.	
			A 2. Nothing to report.	
"	11/6/16		Coy relieved by 55th M.G. Coy. Coy moved to Sailly-le-Sec with the exception of No 3 section who remained back at Carnoy to dig emplacements for overhead fire N of Peronne Rd.	
Sailly-le-Sec	12/6/16		Cleaning up equipment and packing limbers.	
	13/6/16		Tactical Training.	
	14/6/16		"D"	
	15/6/16		"D"	
	16/6/16		Coy moved from Sailly le Sec to Bray	
Bray	17/6/16		Digging emplacements.	
	18/6/16		"D" – S.A.A. taken to Carnoy & sections carrying same to respective dumps.	

1875 Wt. W593/826 1,000,000 4/15 J.B.C. & A. A.D.S.S./Forms/C. 2118.

Instructions regarding War Diaries and Intelligence Summaries are contained in F. S. Regs., Part II. and the Staff Manual respectively. Title Pages will be prepared in manuscript.

WAR DIARY
or
INTELLIGENCE SUMMARY
(Erase heading not required.)

Army Form C. 2118

Place	Date	Hour	Summary of Events and Information	Remarks and references to Appendices
Bray	19/6/16		Sections digging & carrying S.A.A. to Central Depot.	
	20/6/16		No 1 section enters A 2 Sector. Quiet in front line. Meso two rifle grenades fell near right gun. Carnoy shelled during afternoon about 10 shells fell.	
	21/6/16		Nothing to report. Carrying S.A.A. and battle equipment to Carnoy	
	22/6/16		Nothing to report. Work at getting up equipment continued & completed.	
	23/6/16		Very Quiet. Nothing to report.	
	24/6/16		Sector A 2. Guns No 9 & 10 (Kapree Wood) fired 1500 rounds each about 10 p.m. at: junction of (1) Loop & Pommiers trench. (2) Popoff trench	
Grovetown			A 1 Two guns at Brown St & Glasgow Rd relieved about 10-30 p.m. together firing by 54th M.G. Coy. – Guns now in battle positions.	
	25/6/16		No 1 section guns Nos 1 & 2 fired on flanks of raiding party of 8th Batt Suffolks at 12 midnight. Amm. expended 2,500 rnds. No 3 section fired from 10 p.m till 12 m.n. with three guns into Pommiers trench. S.A.A. expended 4,500 rounds.	
	26/6/16		No 3 section fired ten belts per gun at 4-30 p.m and after 10 p.m into Pommiers line. No 1 section did not fire owing to number of patrols out. Amm. expended 12,000 rounds.	

1875 Wt. W593/826 1,000,000 4/15 J.B.C. & A. A.D.S.S./Forms/C. 2118.

Army Form C. 2118

Instructions regarding War Diaries and Intelligence Summaries are contained in F. S. Regs., Part II. and the Staff Manual respectively. Title Pages will be prepared in manuscript.

WAR DIARY
or
INTELLIGENCE SUMMARY
(Erase heading not required.)

Place	Date	Hour	Summary of Events and Information	Remarks and references to Appendices
Grovetown	27/6/16		No 1 Section mounted gun on top of Cooper's St S T F 12 6?1 in 54th Bde area to fire on Kasino Point.	
			No 1 & 2 guns fired on German wire. – S.A.A. expended 3,500 rounds.	
			No 3 Section fired throughout the night on Pommiers Trench – S.A.A. expended 16,000.	
	28/6/16.		No 1 section fired at 11.30 p.m. on German wire. S.A.A. expended 750 rounds.	
			Patrols were out for remainder of the night. No 3 section fired Midnight 27/28 till 2 a.m. & from 10 p.m. till midnight 28th.	
			S.A.A. expended 16,000 rounds.	
	29/6/16.		No 1 Section did not fire owing to gas attack on our part arranged for 10 p.m. and later raiding activity.	
			No 3 Section fired as usual 16,000 rounds.	
			Casualties Pte LILLEY slight not evacuated. 12,000 SAA brought up.	
	30/6/16		No 3 Section fired occasionally during day. No 1 Section did not fire.	
			No 4 Section reached CARNOY at 4.45 p.m. After rest moved to Assembly trench in rear of Royal Berkshire Regt. No 2 Section arrived 9 p.m. moved in rear of NORFOLK Regt.	

[illegible signature]
Major

1875 Wt. W593/826 1,000,000 4/15 J.B.C. & A. A.D.S.S./Forms/C. 2118.

53rd Bde.
18th Div.

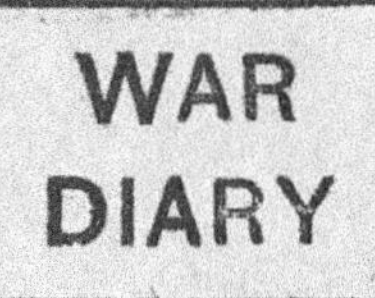

53rd MACHINE GUN COMPANY.

JULY 1916

Battle of the Somme

Attached:-

Report on Operations 23rd June to 21st July.

War Diary

for Month of July 1916

53rd M. G. Coy

Q Map References Throughout
MARICOURT 1/20,000
LONGUEVAL 1/20,000

Instructions regarding War Diaries and Intelligence Summaries are contained in F. S. Regs., Part II. and the Staff Manual respectively. Title Pages will be prepared in manuscript.

WAR DIARY
or
~~INTELLIGENCE SUMMARY~~
(Erase heading not required.)

Army Form C. 2118

Place	Date	Hour	Summary of Events and Information	Remarks and references to Appendices
CARNOY	1/7/16	12.1am	Position of Company No 3 Section 4 guns in position N of PERONNE Rd. firing on Enemy's Pommiers Line. No 1 Section 2 guns in RUSSIAN SAPS Nos 7 & 13. 2 guns in our front line. No 2 Section 4 guns in LEEDS AVENUE with rear company of NORFOLKS. No 4 Section in EDWARDS AVENUE behind Royal BERKSHIRE Regt. Coy HQ. BRICK ALLEY CARNOY. Transport GROVETOWN. No 3 Section fired steadily from midnight	
		7.30	Assault delivered. No 3 Section ceased fire and closed. No 1 Section closed on junction No 4 Assembly trench - CARNOY-MONTAUBAN Rd. Nos 2 & 4 sections (No 2 Section 2/Lt GILBEY 2/Lt SHELDON. No 4 Section 2/Lt GILBERT) advanced with 4 Coys NORFOLKS & BERKS respectively. 2/Lt SHELDON wounded in Berks Support. No 4 Section lost several men in reaching POMMIERS LINE also one gun struck by bullet (Rt side plate) One gun lost later found. Sgt HASLEM wounded in POMMIERS TRENCH	
		8 am	No 3 Section. 2/Lt TULLOCH. closed and ready in BRICK ALLEY. No 1 Section. 2/Lt DAVIDSON. advanced with 10th Bn Essex Regt	
			2 guns No 2 Section in action against LOOP.	
			2 guns No 4 section reached MONTAUBAN ALLEY. a third gun was sent up from No 3 Section also. 2/Lt TOWNSEND reported from GROVETOWN about 5 P.M. and went forward to gun truck with No 1 Section	
		5.45 PM	About this time company was disposed 4 guns No 1 Section (LOOP POMMIERS Trench BUND SUPPORT) 3 guns No 4 Section MONTAUBAN ALLEY and SP 2 A (S26 a 7 6) 3 guns No 3 Section reserve CARNOY 4 guns No 2 section LOOP & LOOP Trench. Later 2 guns No 2 Section moved to CATERPILLAR Trench & NAMELESS Trench (S 26 b)	[signature]

1875 Wt. W593/826 1,000,000 4/15 J.B.C. & A. A.D.S.S./Forms/C. 2118.

Instructions regarding War Diaries and Intelligence Summaries are contained in F. S. Regs., Part II. and the Staff Manual respectively. Title Pages will be prepared in manuscript.

WAR DIARY
or
~~INTELLIGENCE SUMMARY~~

(Erase heading not required.)

Army Form C. 2118

Place	Date	Hour	Summary of Events and Information	Remarks and references to Appendices
CARNOY	2/7/16	11 am	No 1 Section POMMIERS System. Guns moved to strong points 9. LOOP. 13. 15. No 2 Section Gun in NAMELESS trench being very exposed brought into CATERPILLAR trench further N the first gun. 2 guns moved from LOOP to MONTAUBON ALLEY.	
		2 PM	No 3 Section relieved No 4 Section on left front 4 guns in position. 1 SP 2A. 3 in line MONTAUBON ALLEY — BEETLE TRENCH.	
		7 PM	No 4 Section 2 guns relieved to POMMIERS line. (LOOP + SP 6). 2/Lt GREEN reported and reinforced 2/Lt GILBEY 2/Lt TOWNSEND reinforced 2/Lt TULLOCH	
		10.35	DUMP opened at the LOOP.	
	3/7/16		Position of Guns No 2 Section. MONTAUBON ALLEY S26 d 5.4. MONTAUBON ALLEY 26 c 99.30. CATERPILLAR TRENCH S26 d 25.80 ditto S26 b 10.40. Last two guns in action against small parties of enemy E of MAMETZ WOOD. Section commander in liaison with CAPT WOOD Suffolk Regt. No 3 Section - 1 gun Montauban Alley S 26 c 70.45 - 2 guns BEETLE TRENCH S 26 c. 18.42 & 10.50 1 gun SP 2A. In action against small parties of enemy. Section commander in liaison with CAPT BULL Suffolk Regt. Other Sections. Unchanged position	
	4/7/16	-	Position of Guns unchanged save in CATERPILLAR trench where gun was moved forward from S26 d 3.9 to S26 a 99.65. Several targets engaged during day. Observation difficult but obtained on a party at S14 a 7.3.	
	5/7/16	-	Early morning Brigade closed to its right occupying area formerly held by 55 Bde, & being relieved by the 54 Inf Bde. Owing to shorter front No 2 Section (four guns) withdrew to [illegible] in the PERONNE road. No 3 Section occupied four positions in MONTAUBON ALLEY line	

1875 Wt. W593/826 1,000,000 4/15 J.B.C. & A. A.D.S.S./Forms/C. 2118.

Army Form C. 2118

Instructions regarding War Diaries and Intelligence Summaries are contained in F. S. Regs., Part II. and the Staff Manual respectively. Title Pages will be prepared in manuscript.

WAR DIARY
or
~~INTELLIGENCE SUMMARY~~
(Erase heading not required.)

Place	Date	Hour	Summary of Events and Information	Remarks and references to Appendices
CARNOY	5/7/16 contd		No 1 Section 4 guns moved to 4 positions in BACK Trench. No 4 Section (2 guns) remained in LOOP ~~trench~~ till 54 Coy could effect relief.	
		12.50 pm	On relief of No 4 section this section took over No 1 Section four guns & No 1 Section withdrew to billets in CARNOY.	
		6 pm	Position of Coy (1) 4 guns MONTAUBON ALLEY line (No 3 Section) {1. S26 d 50.65, 2. S26 d 80.75, 3. S27 a. 25.90, 4. S27 c. 70.99}	
			barrages of fire (4) BAZENTIN-le-GRAND – MONTAUBON Rd to Pt S16 c 05.95 & the village	
			(2) Road as above to S15 c 60.74	
			(1) Pt S15c 60.74 to S14d 62.72	
			(3) Pt S14a 12.62 and Pt S14b 99.90.	
			18 belts were fired during the day.	
			(2) Four guns in support line	
			(3) Two Sections resting	
			The dump at the LOOP was closed & opened at Pt R2d 77.	
	6/7/16	–	Position of Guns unchanged. 18 belt boxes fired by No 3 Section on barrage lines. 4 new positions sited and lines of fire laid out.	
	7/7/16	–	~~Company relieved by 8 M.G. Coy.~~ No 3 Section fired 3500 rounds along barrage lines.	
			Company relieved by 8 M.G. Coy.	
		4 pm	Nos 1 & 2 sections (resting) moved to BRONFAY FARM.	

1875 Wt. W593/826 1,000,000 4/15 J.B.C. & A. A.D.S.S./Forms/C. 2118.

Army Form C. 2118

Instructions regarding War Diaries and Intelligence Summaries are contained in F. S. Regs., Part II. and the Staff Manual respectively. Title Pages will be prepared in manuscript.

WAR DIARY
or
INTELLIGENCE SUMMARY
(Erase heading not required.)

Place	Date	Hour	Summary of Events and Information	Remarks and references to Appendices
CARNOY	7/7/16	6 PM 8 PM 8 PM	Relief of No 4 Section Complete Relief of No 3 Section Complete Coy HQ moved to BRONFAY FARM	Summary of Events from June 23rd – July 7
BRONFAY FARM	8/7/16	12.30 PM	Coy moved by sections to GROVETOWN CAMP. (S of Junction ALBERT Rd - X Road) BERKS in same camp. ESSEX. SUFFOLKS & NORFOLKS on ALBERT road	Appendices July 1
GROVETOWN	9/7/16	9.30 AM	Section parade. Cleaning Guns Transport moved from Bde Transport lines to lines near Company camp	
— " —	10/7/16	7 AM	Bathing Parade at 7am. Cleaning limbers at 12 to 1.	
— " —	11/7/16	9.30	Tactical training on hills S of Grovetown Camp. No 1 Section 4 guns moved to defence of XIII corps Kite Balloon.	
— " —	12/7/16	9.30	Tactical training on hills S of Grovetown CAMP.	
— " —	13/7/16	9.30	Lecture by Major BAKER CARR. M.G. Corps at 10 am. Staff ride, by CO's adjt etc. MARICOURT to 53 Bde HQ followed by inspection of trenches up to MALTZ HORN FARM.	
	14/7/16	4.30 AM 8 AM	Company moves to BILLON VALLEY. Two guns No 3 Section (2/Lt TULLOCH) with ESSEX to N of BERNAFAY wood. Two guns No 4 Section (2/Lt GILBERT) with SUFFOLKS to S of BERNAFAY WOOD & BRIQUETERIE	

[signature]

1875 Wt. W593/826 1,000,000 4/15 J.B.C. & A. A.D.S.S./Forms/C. 2118.

Instructions regarding War Diaries and Intelligence Summaries are contained in F. S. Regs., Part II. and the Staff Manual respectively. Title Pages will be prepared in manuscript.

WAR DIARY
or
~~INTELLIGENCE SUMMARY~~

(Erase heading not required.)

Army Form C. 2118

Place	Date	Hour	Summary of Events and Information	Remarks and references to Appendices
BILLON VALLEY	14/7/16	8 AM	No 2 Section & 2 guns No 3 Section 2 guns No 4 section (short of teams) in BILLON VALLEY. No 1 Section not yet relieved from Corps balloon. Coy HQ established in SCHOOL St MARICOURT	
MARICOURT		2.26 PM	2 Guns No 3 Section established in Strong Points held by No 6 Company ESSEX Regt on E face of BERNAFAY wood. 2 guns No 4 Section in S.E. corner of BERNAFAY wood. All four guns in SUPPORT positions as TRONES WOOD is held by 5? Bde and the 9th Divn have taken LONGUEVAL	
MARICOURT	15/7/16		Position of Guns unchanged. Defence of Corps balloon taken over by 2 guns No 1 + R gun.	
		5.45 PM	No 4 Section (new draft) 2/Lt [illegible] 2 guns No 1 reached BILLON VALLEY 5.45 PM. Later one gun No 4 section moved to MALTZ HORN Trench	
— " —	16/7/16		Attack on GUILLEMONT planned and positions sighted. This attack postponed at 2 pm. 2 guns No 3 Section and 2 guns No 4 Section relieved by 105 MGC ([illegible] GORDON)	[illegible, crossed out]
		8.15 PM	Relief complete 8.15 pm. Sections returned to BILLON VALLEY	
— " —	17/7/16		Sections resting in BILLON VALLEY. Operations again postponed	
— " —	18/7/16			

1875 Wt. W593/826 1,000,000 4/15 J.B.C. & A. A.D.S.S./Forms/C. 2118.

Instructions regarding War Diaries and Intelligence Summaries are contained in F. S. Regs., Part II. and the Staff Manual respectively. Title Pages will be prepared in manuscript.

WAR DIARY
or
~~INTELLIGENCE~~ SUMMARY
(Erase heading not required.)

Army Form C. 2118

Place	Date	Hour	Summary of Events and Information	Remarks and references to Appendices
MARICOURT	18-7-16	–	Operations against GUILLEMONT postponed. Company relieved from guarding XIII Corps Balloon.	
		10 PM	Stood to, and moved to TALUS BOISÉ following infantry of Brigade	
	19-7-16	1.30 A.M.	Reached TALUS BOISÉ and bivouacked.	
			53rd Inf Bde came under orders of 9th Division and ordered to attack LONGUEVAL & DELVILLE wood (verbal orders at conference MARICOURT CHATEAU 2.00)	
			Company to send one section with each Infantry Battalion.	
			SUFFOLKS to attack village. NORFOLKS to clear wood S of PRINCES St. ESSEX N.E corner of wood. Royal BERKS NW portion	
MONTAUBON	---	2.10 A.M.	Left TALUS BOISÉ with fighting limbers.	
		4.30 A.M.	Reached Brigade rendezvous S22d. unloaded and allotted sections to battalions	
			No 2 Section 2/Lt GREEN & 2/Lt SMALLWOOD to NORFOLKS	
			No 3 " 2/Lt TULLOCH & 2/Lt TOWNSEND to ESSEX	
			No 4 " 2/Lt GILBERT to Royal BERKS	
			No 1 " 2/Lt DAVIDSON to SUFFOLKS	
		7 AM.	No 2 Section left valley & advanced towards village. little barrage at the time.	
			No 3 left at 8.15 No 4 at 8.45 No 1 at 9.30. Infantry advance was very slow and as the barrage increased casualties were sustained. No 1 section lost several	
		10 AM.	men at sunken road at S17c. No 4 section also lost heavily at entrance to village	
			No 2 Section got into wood about noon and moved along SOUTH STREET	
			No 1 into position in the village about 2 o'clock. guns remainder out of action with casualties	
			No 3 & 4 sections blocked in trench S17d till about 4 o'clock when got into wood and into position facing north with fairly good field of fire.	[signature]

1875 Wt. W593/826 1,000,000 4/15 J.B.C. & A. A.D.S.S./Forms/C. 2118.

Instructions regarding War Diaries and Intelligence Summaries are contained in F. S. Regs., Part II. and the Staff Manual respectively. Title Pages will be prepared in manuscript.

Army Form C. 2118

WAR DIARY
or
~~INTELLIGENCE SUMMARY~~
(Erase heading not required.)

Place	Date	Hour	Summary of Events and Information	Remarks and references to Appendices
MONTAUBON (LONGUEVAL)	19-7-16	5 P.M.	At this time position was:- one gun No 1 Section S of CLARGES St 4 guns No 2 Section along SOUTH STREET facing S.E. 4 guns No 3 Section between S 18 a (centre) & S 18 b (centre) facing N. 4 guns No 4 Section in S.W. end of wood facing N.W. 2/Lt TOWNSEND had been missing since leaving for reconnaissance at 4 P.M.	
		11 P.M.	After dark guns had been pushed out further. No 2 Section took over abandoned VICKERS at S.E. corner of wood S18 b 1.7 No 3 " moved right hand gun to S18 c. 6.8 (approx). This gun had very good targets No 4 " moved left gun to position opposite church S17 b 8.4 (approx). This gun also fired heavily	
- " -	20-7-16	12.30 am	Guns in wood continually in action against enemy counter attacks, considerable execution presumably done	
		1-10 to 3.30 am	Attack by 76 Bde not successful.	
			20th Fairly quiet. Village and S.W. corner of wood shelled and considerable sniping in wood. 2/Lt TULLOCH seriously wounded. 2/Lt SMALLWOOD wounded	
		evening	Night of 20/21 quiet. few guns fired as patrols were out. All Infantry of Brigade less NORFOLKS - were relieved by 76 Bde 3 Division. No 1 Section relieved and withdrew to S 22 d	
	21-7-16	-	Morning 21-7-16 quiet, little barrage. No further casualties	
		2 P.M.	76 B. M.G. Coy arranged relief 6.30 relief complete	
		7 P.M.	No 2 Section arrived in valley followed No 4 at 7.20 and No 3 2/Lt GILBERT wounded while leaving the village	[illegible]

1875 Wt. W593/826 1,000,000 4/15 J.B.C. & A. A.D.S.S./Forms/C. 2118.

Army Form C. 2118 7

WAR DIARY
or
~~INTELLIGENCE SUMMARY~~
(Erase heading not required.)

Instructions regarding War Diaries and Intelligence Summaries are contained in F. S. Regs., Part II. and the Staff Manual respectively. Title Pages will be prepared in manuscript.

Place	Date	Hour	Summary of Events and Information	Remarks and references to Appendices
MONTAUBON (LONGUEVAL)	21-7-16	7·30	Section moved off from valley S22 d to rendezvous at BILLON	Appendix
		~~7·30~~ 8am 10PM	Limbers up from TALUS BOISE, ~~to~~ to S22d loaded up and returned to BILLON	Return of horses etc 19-7-16 to 21-7-16
		10PM	Coy HQ to BILLON VALLEY	"July (1)"

[signature]

1875 Wt. W593/826 1,000,000 4/15 J.B.C. & A. A.D.S.S./Forms/C. 2118.

Instructions regarding War Diaries and Intelligence Summaries are contained in F. S. Regs., Part II. and the Staff Manual respectively. Title Pages will be prepared in manuscript.

WAR DIARY
or
~~INTELLIGENCE~~ SUMMARY
(Erase heading not required.)

Army Form C. 2118

Place	Date	Hour	Summary of Events and Information	Remarks and references to Appendices
GROVETOWN	22-7-16	2 AM	Co. HQ opened at GROVETOWN	
		5 AM	Transport reached GROVETOWN	
		8 AM	Section left independently for MERICOURT station. 9.30 AM Transport left by road for LONGPRÉ	
TRAIN		11 AM	Company arrived MERICOURT station	
		2.30 PM	Entrained. Reached LONGPRÉ	
LONGPRÉ (sur Somme)	—"—			
—"—	23-7-16		Resting at LONGPRÉ	
	afternoon		Transport arrived and parked	
—"—	24-7-16	9.40	Transport at station LONGPRÉ	
		11.15	Company parade for entrainment for North. Entrained with Bde HQ. Bde Signal Coy & 58 TM. Bty	
			Reached ARQUES. Detrained and marched to BLAIRINGHEM. (Pas de Calais) arrived 11 PM	
BLAIRINGHEM	25-7-16		Resting at BLARINGHEM.	
—"—	26-7-16		Cleaning Guns etc	
	27-7-16	9.30 am	Company Parade under C.S.M. Dickinson for drill & rifle exercise	
	28-7-16	11.30	Parade lecture on anti-gas appliances by Sgt. Stretton	[signature] Major

1875 Wt. W593/826 1,000,000 4/15 J.B.C. & A. A.D.S.S./Forms/C. 2118.

Instructions regarding War Diaries and Intelligence Summaries are contained in F. S. Regs., Part II. and the Staff Manual respectively. Title Pages will be prepared in manuscript.

WAR DIARY
or
~~INTELLIGENCE SUMMARY~~
(Erase heading not required.)

Army Form C. 2118

9

Place	Date	Hour	Summary of Events and Information	Remarks and references to Appendices
BLAIRINGHEM	29-7-16	4 AM	Company Paraded for move. Bde moved by route march to GUEDEWAERSWELD via WALLON CAPPEL & HAZEBROUCK	
		10 AM	Reached GUEWAERS WELDE	
GODEWAERS-WELD				
— " —	30-7-16		Resting in billets	
— " —	31-7-16		Training Gun Drill and Mechanism. 2/Lt R.J. GREEN transferred to 24 M.G. Co. 2/Lts BEDDALL CAESAR BROWN from England.	

John R. Dan...
Major

Instructions regarding War Diaries and Intelligence Summaries are contained in F. S. Regs., Part II. and the Staff Manual respectively. Title Pages will be prepared in manuscript.

Army Form C. 2118

~~WAR DIARY~~
or
INTELLIGENCE SUMMARY
(Erase heading not required.)

APPENDIX:
"JULY (1)

Place	Date	Hour	Summary of Events and Information				Remarks and references to Appendices
			Approximate No of Rounds Fired.	Guns out of Action.	Casualties		
CARNOY–MONTAUBON	July 1st		19.500	1 (permanent rifle bullet)	1 Officer	13 OR 4 " attached.	
"	June 24th – July 8th.		124.500	– " –	1 Officer.	16 OR 8 attached	
LONGUEVAL – DELVILLE WOOD	July 19 – July 22		19.000	3 (temporarily) casualties to personnel 1 (temporarily) broken fuzee spring	4 officers	26 OR. 32 attached (about)	

[signature]
Major

1875 Wt. W593/826 1,000,000 4/15 J.B.C. & A. A.D.S.S./Forms/C. 2118.

FROM O.C. 53 M.G. Coy.

TO. 53 Inf. Bde.

Herewith I beg to submit report on fighting 23rd June to 21 July 1916 in so far as the company under my command was affected.

John R. Bentley [signature]
Major.

30-7-16.

Seen
[illegible]

Report on Fighting.
53rd Machine Gun Company.

1. **First Period. 23rd June – July 1st.**

During the preliminary stage the company was disposed with one section in the line, one section N. of the Peronne Road doing overhead fire, and two sections resting. The company had been fortunate in being able to get a large amount of work done before 'U' day particularly on the four gun emplacements N of Peronne Road, where No 3 Section had done very well. The security thus gained amply repayed all work, in fact the salient feature of the preliminary stage was the great advantage the company derived both in the front line and the Peronne Rd from the good dug outs provided.

The guns on the Peronne Road fired steadily on the enemy's Pommiers Line system, the guns in the front line, on the enemy's front line wire. This latter only in the rare intervals of patrolling. The guns fired well, and considering the extremely large expenditure of ammunition on the part of No 3 Section, the freedom from mechanical trouble was very creditable. Several gib springs broke but were readily replaced, a broken fuzee spring was also replaced, a later recurrence of this formerly rare stoppage, suggests an inferiority of the present springs. The traversing dial proved a success.

All depots for the assault were ready before 'U' day, and equipment for the assaulting sections Nos 2 & 4 had by that time been taken into position & arranged by O.C.'s sections.

2. **Second Period. The assault of July 1st till July 7th.**

The general scheme of the action of the company was

that one section (No 3) should continue overhead fire until the assault developed. Two sections Nos 2 & 4 should advance with the two assaulting battalions, one section No 1 with the supporting battalion. On the whole the scheme worked well, though it would appear that the guns need not have advanced so early. Even with the fourth company of the assault they were very soon close up behind the assaulting lines, & were exposed to various fires to which they could not reply. In spite of the very able leadership of 2/Lt Gilbert No 4 section lost heavily in personnel & had one gun damaged without having been able to come into action. On the right 2 guns, No 2 section, 2/Lt Gilbey, fired on the Loop when the Norfolk advance was held up. In general, methods of carrying proved satisfactory, though the box respirator was found to be very inconvenient. Carrying parties were obtained for both assaulting sections and proved indispensable.

By night-fall both sections had established emplacements in, & N of, Montauban Alley, at first for defensive purposes. The following day guns were pushed further forward particularly down Caterpillar trench, and some firing was done. There was still however considerable doubt as to the tactical situation on the left which was not cleared up till midday. From then onwards guns fired fairly heavily at long ranges onto German second line between Bazentin-le Grand village and Bazentin-le Petit wood, also on the road at S 14 a. On two occasions with a powerful telescope observation was obtained at 2500 yds. For the rest, as the German trenches were heavily manned considerable loss was probably caused. On the 5 July the Brigade closed to its right permitting the relief of one section, but otherwise without affecting the situation, save that the advance of our infantry in the areas of Marlborough Wood, Mametz Wood, rendered firing West of North difficult. The difficulties of rationing providing ammunition etc consequent on having the whole company in the line were now lessened and No 3 section fired heavily.

On 8th the company was relieved and returned to Grovetown.

3. Third Phase 14th July - 16 July both inclusive.

3. The third phase consisted of the supporting operations in the vicinity of BERNAFAY WOOD. The two sections involved Nos 3 & 4. ~~very~~ were in positions very exposed to shell fire but were able, partly to find good German dugouts, partly to dig strong trenches with the result that casualties were comparatively light. During this period the attack on GUILLEMONT was planned, an operation offering great opportunities for Machine Gun fire, positions having been found for six guns to do semi-observed overhead fire. This period came to

4. an end with the withdrawal of all sections to BILLON VALLEY evening 16 July.

4 Fourth Phase. The Attack on LONGUEVAL and DELVILLE WOOD.

Owing to the extremely unfavourable nature of the ground and the rapidity with which preparations for the attack were pushed forward, the company ~~went~~ went into action one section with each battalion of the Brigade. Under ~~the~~ circumstances ~~the~~ which could hardly be avoided ~~but~~ ~~would~~ the guns and teams were for a long time in ~~position~~ the open, exposed to heavy shell fire & unable to reply. It was not till midday to late afternoon that the guns got into position. - No 2 section on the south of the wood, No 3 the centre facing North, No 4 the eastern edge and No 1, three of whose guns were out of action owing to casualties, in the village of LONGUEVAL. At nightfall No 3 section pushed further to the right and covered the N.W. front of our lines in the wood, No 2 section in addition to its own guns assisted the infantry to man an

d/c

- No 1 Section 2/Lt DAVIDSON
No 3 Section - 2/Lt TULLOCH.
No 2 Section 2/Lt GREEN.

abandoned Vickers gun at the S.E. angle of the wood, and No 4 section sent a gun up to the important point S17684. During all the confused fighting which followed gun commanders appear to have shown considerable initiative, and to have inflicted considerable loss on the enemy. Heavy losses in officers and other ranks were experienced during this period. The company was fortunate that on relief on 21st it was able to bring out its complete equipment of sixteen guns and tripods intact ~~complete~~. During this phase carrying parties of four men per gun were provided from battalions and proved to be no more than was absolutely necessary. Cooperation with the infantry was good throughout. With all the fighting strength of the company in the line some difficulty was experienced in getting up water & rations. Fortunately there was a large amount of ammunition lying about the wood from which empty belts were filled. One broken fuzee spring was the only mechanical trouble.

No 4 Section

2/Lt Gilbert.

It may be worth noting that a large amount of ammunition was lying about in Lewis drums. As ~~at~~ the drums are at present built this ammunition is very difficult to get out for use in rifles or machine guns.

On July 21st the Company was relieved and returned to GROVETOWN.

General Notes.

In general the fighting seemed to emphasise the following points. The guns themselves, given proper attention, will stand any amount of wear. The mechanical and tactical training of the crews appears to have been along correct lines, & to have been sufficient. The leading of the officers was gallant in the extreme. For the first 24 hours after the assault a proper grasp of what could be done under the new conditions was partially absent. This was probably assisted by the fact that in expectation of rough trouble fighting telescopes and range finders had been left behind. After this had been pointed out, all targets ~~Range finders carrying Parties ~~ were vigorously engaged.

Carrying parties are absolutely essential.

However boldly led, the Vickers gun cannot be considered a weapon of assault. On the move it is vulnerable to bombers, snipers, as well as to the ordinary accidents of shell fire. Therefore it appears that the Vickers guns which are going forward to take up positions in the consolidated line, should ~~move~~ start as late as possible and should move as rapidly as possible to the new positions.

As far as can be seen from past experience there is no reason why the advance of the Vickers guns with perhaps a small escort, should not be entirely independent of the infantry advance.

In future better cooperation with the artillery might with advantage be obtained

[signature]

Major

O.C. 53rd Machine Gun Company.

July 30th 1916.

53rd Coy

M.G.C.

War Diary

for

August 1916.

53rd Machine Gun Company.

Major

O.C. 53 M.G. Coy

Army Form C. 2118 1

Instructions regarding War Diaries and Intelligence Summaries are contained in F. S. Regs., Part II. and the Staff Manual respectively. Title Pages will be prepared in manuscript.

WAR DIARY

or

~~INTELLIGENCE SUMMARY~~

(Erase heading not required.)

Place	Date	Hour	Summary of Events and Information	Remarks and references to Appendices
GODWAERSWELDE	1/8/16	8.30 AM 2.30 PM	Company Parade in Transport Lines Inspection by Major General commanding 18th Division	
— " —	2/8/16		Training near billets	
— " —	3/8/16		Training near billets	
— " —	4/8/16		Training near billets. 2/Lt R. G. Davidson and Cpl Hall. left for ESTAIRES billeting party	
— " —	5/8/16	4 AM.	Company paraded for march to ESTAIRES. Route METEREN & OUDESTEENE. Arrived about 9.30. No men fell out. Rear party Lt. WILLIAMS & 6 O.R. came in 12.30 p.m. 3 P.M. Company at 61st Divisional baths.	
ESTAIRES	6/8/16	—	Resting in Billets. Church Services 10 AM 11.15 AM & 7 PM	
— " —	7/8/16	—	Resting in Billets. 2/Lt Gilbey. Cpl Hall left for ERQUINGHEM as billeting party.	
— " —	8/8/16	4.45 AM	Company paraded for march to ERQUINGHEM Route FERME de BRETAGNE - CROIX de BAC Reached billets about 10 AM	
ERQUINGHEM	9/8/16	—	O.C. Visited sector held by 54th Inf Bde neighbourhood of RUE du BOIS. S.E. of ARMENTIERES Sector almost entirely breastwork. Situation Quiet. Major MATHESON 54 M.G.C., guiding, wounded	
— " —	10/8/16	—	O.C. Company & 2/Lt BEDDALL visited sector held by 55th Inf. Bde in front of BOIS GRENIER Quiet.	
— " —	11/8/16	—	Resting in Billets.	
— " —	12/8/16	6.45 AM	Company paraded for march to BAILLEUL (MONT de LILLE). Reached camp about 9.30 Whole brigade in large camp in training area S.E. of town.	
BAILLEUL	13/8/16	10. AM	Church Parade in camp.	

[signature]
Major

1875 Wt. W593/826 1,000,000 4/15 J.B.C. & A. A.D.S.S./Forms/C. 2118.

Army Form C. 2118

Instructions regarding War Diaries and Intelligence Summaries are contained in F. S. Regs., Part II. and the Staff Manual respectively. Title Pages will be prepared in manuscript.

WAR DIARY
or
~~INTELLIGENCE SUMMARY~~
(Erase heading not required.)

Place	Date	Hour	Summary of Events and Information	Remarks and references to Appendices
BAILLEUL	14/8/16		Training in neighbourhood of MONT de LILLE	
		12.20 P.M.	Visit to training area of H.M. The KING.	
			2/Lt EVANS to Machine Gun School CAMIERS	
			2/Lt BROWN to two lectures (14th & 15th inst.) at WISQUES 2nd Army School	
— " —	15/8/16	8 – Am – 12.30 P.M.	Training around camp	
— " —	16/8/16	— " —	Training around camp	
— " —	17/8/16	7. Am	Route march with 8 B. SUFFOLK Regt. route VIEUX-BERQUIN & OUDERSTEENE	
— " —	18/8/16	—	Wet weather interfered with training. O.C. Company to lecture by Major BAKER-CARR at 2nd Army School WISQUES on LEWIS GUNS.	
— " —	19/8/16	—	Wet weather interfered with training	
— " —	20/8/16	–	Church parade 10 Am	
— " —	21/8/16	8 am 12.30 P.M	Training around camp. Visit of G.O.C. 2nd A.N.Z.A.C. Corps	
— " —	22.8.16	8 – am 12.30 P.M	Training around camp	
— " —	23.8.16	"	— " —	
— " —	24.8.16	"	— " —	

[signature] Major

1875 Wt. W593/826 1,000,000 4/15 J.B.C. & A. A.D.S.S./Forms/C. 2118.

Army Form C. 2118

Instructions regarding War Diaries and Intelligence Summaries are contained in F. S. Regs., Part II. and the Staff Manual respectively. Title Pages will be prepared in manuscript.

WAR DIARY
or
~~INTELLIGENCE SUMMARY~~
(Erase heading not required.)

Place	Date	Hour	Summary of Events and Information	Remarks and references to Appendices
BAILLEUL	25-8-16	2.55 am	Parade for entrainment at BAILLEUL Main Station. Transport arrived 3.5 am	
		6.24	Departure of train. Route via HAZEBROUCK LILLERS & CHOQUES.	
		9.46	Arrival of train. Detrained at DIEVAL, marched via BAJUS & FREVILLERS to VILLERS-BRULIN arrived in billets 1.30 PM	
VILLERS-BRULIN	26/8-16	–	Resting in billets. Training areas visited by OC Coy	
– " –	27/8/16	–	No 2 Section training with 8th NORFOLKS at BOIS des HERONBUS. Other sections training near billets.	
– " –	28/8/16	–	All sections save No 2 firing on range 6.30 am – 1 PM. OC Coy with COs of Inf. Bn & Bde Majors 54 & 53 Bdes visited TRENCH LINE of XVII Corps. NEUVILLE . St VAASTE – ECURIE	
– " –	29/8/16	–	Bde Operations on Monchy-Breton training area No 2 MG Section with attack Nos 1 & 3 with defence.	
– " –	30/8/16	–	Training in conjunction with 8 Bn Suffolk Regt	
– " –	31/8/16	–	Training in conjunction with 6 Bn Royal Berkshire Regt	

[signature] Major

1875 Wt. W593/826 1,000,000 4/15 J.B.C. & A. A.D.S.S./Forms/C. 2118.

vol 7

War Diary for

September 1916.

of 53rd M. G. Company.

[illegible] Major

O. 53 M.G.C.

4-10-16.

From. O.C. 53 M.G. Coy.

To H.Q. 53rd I/Bde.

Herewith WAR DIARY for SEPTEMBER for Unit under my command.

M.G.C 459
4-10-16.

[signature]
Major

53 12. C. Coy

Instructions regarding War Diaries and Intelligence Summaries are contained in F. S. Regs., Part II. and the Staff Manual respectively. Title Pages will be prepared in manuscript.

WAR DIARY

or

~~INTELLIGENCE SUMMARY~~

(Erase heading not required.)

Army Form C. 2118

1

Place	Date	Hour	Summary of Events and Information	Remarks and references to Appendices
VILLERS-BRULIN	1 Sept	8.30 AM - 1.0 PM	Company Training over MONCHY-BRETON area in association with 8 SUFFOLKS.	
"	2 Sept	8.30 - 1.0 PM	Training on MONCHY-BRETON area in association with 8 Norfolks No targets available at range	
"	3 Sept	7.30 PM	BRIGADE OPERATIONS Nos 2 & 4 Section under Lt G. E Falkner with the attack. Nos 1 & 3 Sections under OC Coy attached to defence under Col. CLAY 6 R Berks. Returned to billets 3.30 PM Lt M.C DAVIDSON on Special leave to ENGLAND.	
"	4 Sept	2 AM.	Parade for repetition of Bde Operation as a dawn attack. Dispositions as for attack on 3rd Sept. Lt G.E. FALKNER to REBREUVE for billeting	
"	5 Sept	-	Preparations for move to REBREUVE cancelled in early morning. Training near billets	
"	6 Sept	-	Training with ESSEX in afternoon. Class for NCOs & No 1s under 2/Lt GILBEY	
"	7 Sept	"	Exhibition of Intensive Digging	
"	8 Sept		Exhibition of Intensive Digging. Company bathed at TINQUES	John [illegible] Major

1875 Wt. W593/826 1,000,000 4/15 J.B.C. & A. A.D.S.S./Forms/C. 2118.

53 M.G. C

Instructions regarding War Diaries and Intelligence Summaries are contained in F. S. Regs., Part II. and the Staff Manual respectively. Title Pages will be prepared in manuscript.

WAR DIARY
or
INTELLIGENCE SUMMARY
(Erase heading not required.)

Army Form C. 2118

2

Place	Date	Hour	Summary of Events and Information	Remarks and references to Appendices
VILLERS-BRULIN	9-9-16	7AM	Coy left VILLERS-BRULIN for REBREUVE. Route TINQUES-PENIN-AMBRINES-MAGNICOURT HOUVIN-HOUVIGNEUL.	
REBREUVE		4PM	Arrived billets REBREUVE. 3 Casualties	
	10-9-16	8AM	Coy left REBREUVE for GROUCHES. route REBREUVIETTE. LE SOUICH. LUCHEUX.	
		12 NOON	Arrived in billets GROUCHES No casualties.	
GROUCHES	11-9-16	6.[illegible]am	Coy left GROUCHES for LEALVILLERS. Route. HALLOY. THIEVRES. AUTHIE. LOUVENCOURT	
LEALVILLERS		12.7[illegible]	Arrived in billets LEALVILLERS. No casualties	
LEALVILLERS	12-9-16	–	Resting in billets	
– " –	13-9-16	–	Training on Area S of CLAIRFAIX	
– " –	14-9-16	–	Training on Area	
– " –	15-9-16	–	Training on Area (1 Section) and digging (intensive digging) with 3 Sections on digging ground N.W. of village. Lt M.C. DAVIDSON back from leave.	
– " –	16-9-16	–	Training. About noon orders received to move to BOUZINCOURT. Coy ready to move by 2.30. About to move at 4 when order cancelled.	
– " –	17-9-16	5.55	Moved to BOUZINCOURT. ROUTE ACHEUX. FORCEVILLE. HEDAUVILLE.	Major

1875 Wt. W593/826 1,000,000 4/15 J.B.C. & A. A.D.S.S./Forms/C. 2118.

53 M.G. Coy

Army Form C. 2118

3

Instructions regarding War Diaries and Intelligence Summaries are contained in F. S. Regs., Part II. and the Staff Manual respectively. Title Pages will be prepared in manuscript.

WAR DIARY
or
INTELLIGENCE SUMMARY
(Erase heading not required.)

Place	Date	Hour	Summary of Events and Information	Remarks and references to Appendices
BOUZINCOURT	~~1.25 P.M.~~ 18/9/16	1.25 P.M.	Coy moved to ~~FOR~~FORCEVILLE today. Very wet march.	
FORCEVILLE	19/9/16	-	Resting in billets.	
FORCEVILLE	20/9/16	-	Training in billets & on ground E of village	
— " —	21/9/16	-	Presentation of honours and awards for SOMME Fighting, to 33 Inf Bde on CLAIRFAIX training area by ~~Capt~~ Col RIDDELL for G.O.C. Division. Recipients for 53 M.G. Coy Sgt CROOKES, Cpl BESWICK, L/Cpl ROBINS (Sgt HASLAM in England)	
— " —	22/9/16	"	Company training near billets. O.C. Coy Lt M.C. DAVIDSON & 2/Lt BROWN visited trenches in sectors of 33 Bde & 147 Bde. (DANUBE Tr. HINDENBURG Tr. WONDER WORK)	
— " —	23/9/16	"	Company training near billets. Meeting at ~~[illegible]~~ AVELUY Chateau 5 PM. of M.G. Coy Commanders of 2nd Corps to arrange cooperation	
— " —	24/9/16	"	2/Lts CAESAR & BROWN visit trenches. Second meeting at ~~[illegible]~~ AVELUY Chateau at 4 o'clock for final arrangements for long range ~~fire~~ machine gun fire.	
— " —	25/9/16	"	No 3 & 4 Section moved at 9 AM to DUMBARTON CASTLE (Nr AUTHUILE WOOD) No 1 & 2 Section moved at 10 AM to AUTHUILE Wood. Coy HQ established 1 Noon at W.12.b. central. Transport at HEDAUVILLE	John [illegible] Major

1875 Wt. W593/826 1,000,000 4/15 J.B.C. & A. A.D.S.S./Forms/C. 2118.

53 M. G. Coy

54

Army Form C. 2118

Instructions regarding War Diaries and Intelligence Summaries are contained in F. S. Regs., Part II. and the Staff Manual respectively. Title Pages will be prepared in manuscript.

WAR DIARY
or
INTELLIGENCE SUMMARY

(Erase heading not required.)

Place	Date	Hour	Summary of Events and Information	Remarks and references to Appendices
AUTHUILE WOOD	25/9/16	5.5 PM	LOCATION of Coy. 8 guns (3 & 4 Section) in battery at W.6.c.9.8. – W.6.d.2.8. 8 guns at dug outs near Coy H.Q. W.12.b.4.4.	
			2 Guns No 2 Section moved into position of readiness with 8 Suffolks	
–"–	26/9/16		2 Guns No 2 Section moved into position of readiness with 10 ESSEX	
		Noon.	LOCATION of Coy. 8 guns in battery. 2 Guns with SUFFOLKS. 2 Guns with ESSEX. 4 Guns at Coy H.Q.	
			battery fired 22.500 rounds into & beyond THIEPVAL conforming to artillery lifts during assault.	
–"–	–"–	3.30 PM	2 Guns No 1 Section (2/Lt SHOTTER) went up with 79 Field Coy R.E. to form Strong Point.	
–"–	–"–	3.50 PM	No 3 Section dismounted at W.6.d.2.8. & prepared to move further up	
–"–	–"–	11.30 PM	Location 4 guns No 4 in battery. No 3 Section trying to get up TIP ST to WONDER WORK (heavily barraged). 2 Guns in BULGAR Trench about R.25.b.9.2. & R.26.a.2.5. 2 Guns R.26.d.3.4. & R.26.d.5.5. 2 Guns about R.25.d.6.2. (moving up).	
–"–	27/9/16		One gun (25.b.9.2) knocked out 1 killed 2 wounded. 2 Guns from R.25.d.2 moved up into BULGAR Tr. and one gun No 1 Section went into Strong Point.	
			No 3 Section in battery in HINDENBURG Tr.	
		12 noon	4 guns No 3 Section " " "	
		4 PM	2 " No 4 " " "	
			Other 2 guns No 4 Section resting before joining 7 QUEENS	[signature] Major

1875 Wt. W593/826 1,000,000 4/15 J.B.C. & A. A.D.S.S./Forms/C. 2118.

53 M. G. Coy

#5

Instructions regarding War Diaries and Intelligence Summaries are contained in F. S. Regs., Part II. and the Staff Manual respectively. Title Pages will be prepared in manuscript.

WAR DIARY
or
INTELLIGENCE SUMMARY

(Erase heading not required.)

Army Form C. 2118

Place	Date	Hour	Summary of Events and Information	Remarks and references to Appendices
AUTHUILE - WOOD	27/9/16	4.30 PM	No 3 Section fired on flank of 11 Division assault on STUFF Redoubt 10.750 rounds	
		11 PM –	Fired on LUCKY WAY with one gun from battery	
– " –	28/9/16	4 AM		
			2 Gun No 4 Section 2/Lt GILBEY moved off with 7 QUEENS	
	– " –	10.15 AM		
	– " –	1.35 PM	6 Guns from battery fired onto SCHWABEN redoubt till + 3' then for an hour at range of 2800 yds on line R 13. d 9.3 to R 20 b 50.99 expenditure 11000 rounds.	
			8 Guns from 11th Division at R 27 c – R 26 d fired on slopes S of GRANDCOURT from +15' till 1h 15'	
			2 Guns (2/Lt GILBEY) in Dugout to be SCHWABEN Redoubt not clear.	
	– " –	3 PM	2 Guns No (2 Section) (2/Lt BEDDALL) attached to QUEENS &	
	– " –	8 PM	2 Guns (2/Lt Gilbey) & 2 Guns SUFFOLKS moved up to Front line. One Gun of 2/Lt GILBEY struck by shell, 2 m wounded.	
			one gun 2/Lt BEDDALL got detached	
			The 2 guns got into position R 20 c 2.5 & R 20 c 6.4 & came into action against enemy	
	– " –		3 Guns of Battery fired from dusk to dawn on enemy's communication trenches 15-00 rounds	

John K. Dunlop [?] Major

1875 Wt. W593/826 1,000,000 4/15 J.B.C. & A. A.D.S.S./Forms/C. 2118.

53 M. G. Coy.

Instructions regarding War Diaries and Intelligence Summaries are contained in F. S. Regs., Part II. and the Staff Manual respectively. Title Pages will be prepared in manuscript.

WAR DIARY
or
INTELLIGENCE SUMMARY
(Erase heading not required.)

Army Form C. 2118

6

Place	Date	Hour	Summary of Events and Information	Remarks and references to Appendices
AUTHUILE WOOD	29/6/16	10 AM	No 3 Section moved up to THIEPVAL (No 1 Section taking over battery) One gun of this section had broken down at the battery & been replaced from reserve. One gun (Sgt CROOKES) been pushed up to reinforce front line)	
		NOON	Position of Guns 3 in Front line. 3 in THIEPVAL Defences. 6 in Battery 3 damaged. 1 in Reserve	
		4 PM	From about 4 PM onwards heavy fire from BATTERY onto previous barrage lines 13000 rounds	
		5 PM	55 Coy arrived as relief. ~~Section~~ Relief for battery left AUTHUILE WOOD about 8 PM. Sections back at 12 MIDNIGHT & after tea marched to FORCEVILLE arriving about 3 AM.	
— " —	30/9/16		Relief for Nos 3 & 2 & ½ No 4 Section left at 5.30 AM	
— " —	30/9/16	6 AM	Front line heavily bombarded and bombing attack made on EAST SURREYS to left of 2/Lt GILBEY's gun. This gun in action for a considerable time about 6 AM. 2/Lt BEDDALLS Gun received a direct hit. Later Sgt CROOKES gun damaged. Relief complete about 8. Sections back in valley by 10, except 1 gun (2/Lt EVANS) kept by OC 6 R. Berks till situation cleared. This gun came down about 1 PM. Section marched to FORCEVILLE independently.	
FORCEVILLE		11 AM	HQ left AUTHUILE 10.15. Arrived FORCEVILLE 12 AM.	

1875 Wt. W593/826 1,000,000 4/15 J.B.C. & A. A.D.S.S./Forms/C. 2118.

Instructions regarding War Diaries and Intelligence Summaries are contained in F. S. Regs., Part II. and the Staff Manual respectively. Title Pages will be prepared in manuscript.

Army Form C. 2118

WAR DIARY
or
INTELLIGENCE SUMMARY
(Erase heading not required.)

Place	Date	Hour	Summary of Events and Information	Remarks and references to Appendices
			APPENDIX. Battle THIEPVAL-SCHWABEN 26-30 Sept	
			Rounds Fired. 63,000.	
			Casualties to Personnel Officers 1. Lt St. C. DAVIDSON. Wounded (Remained at Duty)	
			O.R. 1 Killed (attached)	
			6 Wounded	
			2 Shock. shell.	
			Casualties to Guns. 1 Destroyed	
			3 Damaged but brought away.	
			1 Broke Down.	
			Captures 1 Machine Gun. Captured and brought away.	
			5 — " — Captured but left in THIEPVAL.	

[signature]
Major.

1875 Wt. W593/826 1,000,000 4/15 J.B.C. & A. A.D.S.S./Forms/C. 2118.

18

Vol 8

War Diary

for October 1916

53rd M G Company

Army Form C. 2118.

Instructions regarding War Diaries and Intelligence Summaries are contained in F. S. Regs., Part II. and the Staff Manual respectively. Title Pages will be prepared in manuscript.

WAR DIARY
or
INTELLIGENCE SUMMARY
(Erase heading not required.)

Place	Date	Hour	Summary of Events and Information	Remarks and references to Appendices
FLUTHUILE WOOD	1-10-16	5.50 AM	Relief for 6 gun THIEPVAL & SCHWABEN redoubt left: 1	
		8.30 AM	Relief by 55 M.G. Coy complete. All sections down by 10.30 except one gun under 2/Lt Evans temporarily detained in reserve by O.C. 6 R. BERKS.	
			Section marched independently to FORCEVILLE	
FORCEVILLE	~~12.3~~ " PM	12.55 PM	H.Q. arrived FORCEVILLE 2/Lt EVANS with last gun arrived about 3 PM	
			Sgt CROOKES gun and ~~Sgt TUBY's~~ Cpl KELLET's gun both hit and destroyed just before leaving SCHWABEN	
– " –	2-10-16	—	In billets at FORCEVILLE	
– " –	3-10-16	1 PM	Transport left by road for LE MEILLARD	
		5.30 PM	Company entrained on motor lorries at FORCEVILLE for LE MEILLARD	
			Transport GITE was near: DOULLENS	
		11.50 PM	~~Reached~~ Company reached LE MEILLARD.	
LE MEILLARD	4-10-16	4 AM	Transport moved off reached LE MEILLARD about 7	
			Company H.Q. LE GRAND MEILLARD FARM	
– " –	5-10-16	-	Resting in BILLETS	
– " –	6-10-16	-	Resting in BILLETS	

2449 Wt. W14957/M90 750,000 1/16 J.B.C. & A. Forms/C.2118/12.

Instructions regarding War Diaries and Intelligence Summaries are contained in F. S. Regs., Part II. and the Staff Manual respectively. Title Pages will be prepared in manuscript.

WAR DIARY
or
INTELLIGENCE SUMMARY
(Erase heading not required.)

Army Form C. 2118.

Place	Date	Hour	Summary of Events and Information	Remarks and references to Appendices
LE MEILLARD	7-10-16	–	Company Mounted Parade & Drill Physical Training	
– " –	8-10-16	–	Sunday resting in billets.	
– " –	9-10-16	–	Elementary Tactical handling	
– " –	10-10-16	–	Tactical Training.	
– " –	11-10-16	–	Tactical Handling. ~~To [illegible] to TARA HILL ALBERT [illegible]~~ ~~Canadian Corps [illegible] Gun Officers [illegible] BRUTENELL [illegible]~~	
– " –	12-10-16		Brigade practice attack on ground between LE MEILLARD and BOISBERGUES. Transport (brigaded) moved to HERISSART	
– " –	13-10-16		Preparing for move. ~~Transport~~ OC Coy to TARA HILL ALBERT to conference of CANADIAN CORPS M.G. officers held by Lt Col BRUTENELL 1st Can M.M.G. Bde. Transport reached ALBERT	
– " –	14-10-16		Two sections Nos 2 & 4 and Company H.Q. left LE MEILLARD at 9.40 am by MOTOR Bus. Arrived ALBERT 1 pm. Conference with Col BRUTENELL 3 pm. arranged relief with MAJOR BALFOUR 8 Can M.G. Coy. Brigade Conference 6 pm. 2 sections and headquarters billeted in ALBERT for the night.	
ALBERT	15-10-16	8 am	2 Sections Nos 2 & 4 left ALBERT for ZOLLERN TR EAST relieving 8 Canadian M.G. Coy.	
		1.00 pm	Nos 1 & 3 Sections arrived from LE MEILLARD in busses. Had dinner in ALBERT	
		3.00 pm	2 Section and Coy H.Q. left ALBERT.	
		4.10 pm	Company HQ took over from 8 Can M.G. Coy in BAILIFF WOOD.	

2449 Wt. W14957/M90 750,000 1/16 J.B.C. & A. Forms/C.2118/12.

Army Form C. 2118.

Instructions regarding War Diaries and Intelligence Summaries are contained in F. S. Regs., Part II. and the Staff Manual respectively. Title Pages will be prepared in manuscript.

WAR DIARY
or
INTELLIGENCE SUMMARY

(Erase heading not required.)

Place	Date	Hour	Summary of Events and Information	Remarks and references to Appendices
BAILIFF WOOD	16-10-16	-	Position of Company (i) Nos 2 & 4 Sections ZOLLERN TR East R 29. a 9. 8 to 4. 8 firing on to ground in R 10. 11 16 & 17 (ii) Nos 1 2 3 sections in Dugouts in LA BOISELLE. (iii) Coy H.Q. BAILIFF WOOD. (iv) Transport 'Amphitheatre' ALBERT.	
– " –	17-10-16	-	Situation unchanged. Targets engaged as above, also the line R17 d 1.5 to R17 d 3.8 to R.18.a.00 Three men killed and one wounded by chance shell in ZOLLERN TR Night 17-18. 2 guns moved forward to ~~front~~ line to fire on wire in front of REGINA TR 20 Mine frames taken up to ZOLLERN TR and work started on the dugouts.	
POZIERES CEMETARY	18-10-16	-	Situation unchanged. Targets engaged as above but guns not moved forward Company advanced H.Q established at R.34.d.2.5	
– " –	19-10-16	5 AM	No 3 Section left LA BOISELLE for R29 central. Reached there at 8.30. Operations postponed so returned to BOISELLE. Fire programme carried out as usual, very difficult owing to bad weather conditions two guns damaged shrapnel through barrel casing	
– " –	20-10-16	-	Situation unchanged. 20 more mine frames taken up to ZOLLERN TRENCH and put in 32nd Machine Gun Company comes today under orders of G.O.C. 53rd Inf Bde	
– " –	21-10-16	8 AM	No 1 Section relieved No 2 Section in ZOLLERN TR. No 3 Section moved up to R29 in the[?] from there, 2 guns 2/Lt CHESAR moved to 8 NORFOLKS 2 guns 2/Lt HALL to 10 ESSEX	

2449 Wt. W14957/M90 750,000 1/16 J.B.C. & A. Forms/C.2118/12.

Army Form C. 2118

Instructions regarding War Diaries and Intelligence Summaries are contained in F. S. Regs., Part II. and the Staff Manual respectively. Title Pages will be prepared in manuscript.

WAR DIARY
or
INTELLIGENCE SUMMARY
(Erase heading not required.)

Place	Date	Hour	Summary of Events and Information	Remarks and references to Appendices
POZIERES CEMETARY	21-10-16	9.15 am	2 Section 32 M.G. Coy moved to ZOLLERN TR to assist in barrage. H.Q. and 2 sections 32 M.G. Coy moved to dugouts in LA BOISELLE. ATTACK on REGINA TRENCH	
		12.5 PM	16 guns in ZOLLERN trench opened indirect fire at Zero on line of RAVINE in R11. 10 and 16. 2 guns 2/Lt CAESAR went over with NORFOLKS. One knocked out by casualties, other got into position in REGINA TR. 2 guns 2/Lt HALL took up positions in VANCOUVER TR	
			Evening. at request of OC NORFOLKS & OC ESSEX two guns No 1 Section moved to REGINA, right half. 2 guns 32 M.G. Company moved to REGINA, left half (Norfolks). Casualties in attack 1 O.R. killed 5 wounded	
– " –	22.10.16	–	Situation in REGINA Quiet. 1 gun No 1 Section (Sgt BURKILL) fired several bursts	
		10 AM	No 4 section withdrew from ZOLLERN TR leaving 8 guns there (6 32 Coy 2 53 Company)	
			Afternoon one remaining gun 2/Lt CAESAR hit by shell. 2/Lt SHOTTER. 2 guns No 1 Section moved up to relieve him. Relief delayed by shelling. One gun team No 2 Section brought up to Coy HQ from BOISELLE	
– " –	23.10.16	5 AM	2/Lt CAESAR with one team back to R29 central	
		–	54 M.G. Coy relieved 53 M.G. Coy in the line during the day, taking over 4 guns in REGINA Tr. and placing four guns in reserve. Relief delayed by congestion and shelling. Last gun team out by 6 PM. H.Q. and 2 Section to ALBERT. No 1 Section and half No 3 Section slept the night in dugouts at LA BOISELLE. 2 Sections 32 M.G. Coy remained in ZOLLERN Tr to do indirect fire. OC 53 M.G. Coy remained up also.	
ALBERT	24.10.16	–	All sections moved in to ALBERT by 10 AM. billeted in RUE de DOULLENS.	

1875 Wt. W593/826 1,000,000 4/15 J.B.C. & A. A.D.S.S./Forms/C. 2118.

Army Form C. 2118.

Instructions regarding War Diaries and Intelligence Summaries are contained in F. S. Regs., Part II. and the Staff Manual respectively. Title Pages will be prepared in manuscript.

WAR DIARY
or
INTELLIGENCE SUMMARY
(Erase heading not required.)

Place	Date	Hour	Summary of Events and Information	Remarks and references to Appendices
ALBERT	25/10/16	-	Company resting in ALBERT.	
—"—	26/10/16	-	Company moved to No 5 Rue de CORBIE. (over RUE de CORBIE BATHS).	
—"—	27/10/16	-	Resting in ALBERT	
—"—	28/10/16	-	Resting in ALBERT.	
—"—	29/10/16	-	Company relieved 32nd M.G. Coy. Nos 3 & 4 Sections relieved two sections in ZOLLERN Trench. Nos 1 & 2 Sections moved to LA BOISELLE. Headquarters at LA BOISELLE.	
—"—	30/10/16	—	Fire programme at 16,400 rounds per day carried out on ravine and ground in 10d. & 11.c.d. & b.	
—"—	31/10/16	-	Nos 1 & 2 Sections relieved Nos 3 & 4. in ZOLLERN TRENCH. Programme continued.	

[signature]
Major
OC 53 MG C.

2449 Wt. W14957/M90 750,000 1/16 J.B.C. & A. Forms/C.2118/12.

Instructions regarding War Diaries and Intelligence Summaries are contained in F. S. Regs., Part II. and the Staff Manual respectively. Title Pages will be prepared in manuscript.

WAR DIARY
or
INTELLIGENCE SUMMARY

(Erase heading not required.)

Army Form C. 2118.

Place	Date	Hour	Summary of Events and Information	Remarks and references to Appendices

2449 Wt. W14957/M90 750,000 1/16 J.B.C. & A. Forms/C.2118/12.

Vol 9

War Diary

for month of November 1916

53rd M. G. Coy

[illegible] Major

Instructions regarding War Diaries and Intelligence Summaries are contained in F. S. Regs., Part II. and the Staff Manual respectively. Title Pages will be prepared in manuscript.

WAR DIARY
or
INTELLIGENCE SUMMARY

(Erase heading not required.)

Army Form C. 2118.

Place	Date	Hour	Summary of Events and Information	Remarks and references to Appendices
POZIERES	1/11/16	–	Company relieved 54th M.G. Coy. in the line. No 1 Section relieved 3 guns in VANCOUVER TR. R.23.b.6.3, R 23b 84 & R 23d.0.5. No 2 Section relieved 3 guns in REGINA TR. R17 b 2 3. & two guns at R.23.a.5.6. Both these sections moved forward from ZOLLERN TR. One gun team of each section moved to reserve dugouts near the BELL". 1 Section 54th M.G. Coy, & 1 Section 53 M.G. Coy took over indirect fire from ZOLLERN TR.	
		11AM	Coy HQ moved to the 'BELL' dugout 'Centre Way'. Guns in REGINA withdraw to ZOLLERN by day.	
	2/11/16	–	No 3 & 4 Sections relieved Nos 2 & 1 Sections respectively. Nos 1 & 2 Sections returned to dugouts in LA BOISELLE. Transport took 16 boxes SAA by pack mule to ZOLLERN TR after dark. Area kept under fire from ZOLLERN TR. (i) R10d 3.7. to 9.9. (ii) R11 c 1.4 to 8.4 (iii) R11c. 8.6 to 11d.4.5. (iv) R11 d 4.9. to 12 c.1.9 also area 19 b 99 to 12 c 05.	
	3/11/16	–	Ordinary firing. Nothing to report. Lt WALLACE from 97 M.G Coy reported as 2nd in Command vice Lt FALKNER (to 19 M.G Coy as C.O.)	
	4/11/16	–	Nos 1 & 2 Sections relieved No 2 & 4 Section. No 1 ~~moved~~ arrived at ZOLLERN TR at 1 p.m. and moved forward to REGINA TR at dusk. No 2 Section reached VANCOUVER TR at 12 midday. Transport took 20 boxes up to ZOLLERN just before dawn.	
	5/11/16	–	Company (less 1 Section) relieved in line by 52 M.G. Coy. No 2 Section moved to ZOLLERN TR and came under orders of O.C. 52 M.G. Coy. Remaining sections moved to ALBERT. Nos 3 & 4 from BOISELLE, No 1 from the line, & Hq from POZIERES.	

2449 Wt. W14957/M90 750,000 1/16 J.B.C. & A. Forms/C.2118/12.

Instructions regarding War Diaries and Intelligence Summaries are contained in F. S. Regs., Part II. and the Staff Manual respectively. Title Pages will be prepared in manuscript.

WAR DIARY
or
INTELLIGENCE SUMMARY
(Erase heading not required.)

Army Form C. 2118.

Place	Date	Hour	Summary of Events and Information	Remarks and references to Appendices
ALBERT	5/11/16	12 noon	O.C. 52 M.G. Coy took over defence of sector. Company in billets RUE de CORBIE.	
– " –	6/11/16	—	Cleaning and repacking limbers.	
– " –	7/11/16	—	No 3 Section relieved No 2 Section in the line. leaving ALBERT at 9 a.m. Sgt JOBY. Cpl. WALTON Pte BARNES were presented with ribbon of the Military Medal at a Brigade Parade at WARLOY, by G.O.C. 18 Division.	
– " –	8/11/16	—	Company resting in billets in ALBERT	
– " –	9/11/16	—	Company resting in billets in ALBERT	
– " –	10/11/16	10.30 PM	No 4 Section left ALBERT proceeding to POZIERES by bus and thence to REGINA TR No 1 Section similarly proceeded to VANCOUVER TR	
– " –	11/11/16	—	Company relieved 56 Company in the line. Similarly 32nd M.G. Coy which the orders of 53 Inf. Bde. relieved 55th M.G. Coy in the MOUQUET FARM SECTOR	
		7 AM	Coy. HQ. established at the "BELL"	
		~~[illegible]~~ 4.20 AM	Nos 1 & 4 Sections completed relief of 54 M.G. Coy	
		10 AM	No 2 section relieved No 3 section in ZOLLERN TR. Position of Guns etc: R.18.c.2.3 R.23.a.4.6 (2). R.23.c.4.2 (ANTI AEROPLANE) R.23.c.6.4. (ANTI AEROPLANE) R.23.c.7.4 at R.29.a.0.8 (4) at CENTRE WAY 2 in reserve (one mounted ANTI AEROPLANE)	

2449 Wt. W14957/M90 750,000 1/16 J.B.C. & A. Forms/C.2118/12.

Instructions regarding War Diaries and Intelligence Summaries are contained in F. S. Regs., Part II. and the Staff Manual respectively. Title Pages will be prepared in manuscript.

WAR DIARY
or
INTELLIGENCE SUMMARY

(Erase heading not required.)

Army Form C. 2118.

Place	Date	Hour	Summary of Events and Information	Remarks and references to Appendices
POZIERES	12/11/16	-	Nothing to report, usual programme of fire carried out. 16 boxes SAA brought up by transport. One O.R. wounded	
			- One section 32nd MG Coy ordered to ZOLLERN TR to support attack of 19 Division on 13th	
		10 P.M.	Section 32 MG Coy passed CENTRE WAY	
	13/11/16	12.30 AM	No 3 Section (2/Lt HALL) reached BELL dugout CENTRE WAY, & bivouaced in dugouts in the neighbourhood, except 3 men who proceeded to REGINA TR (right hand gun) to relieve Cpl HALLIDAY.	
		4.45 AM	Cpl HALLIDAY's team arrived back at the BELL	
		6.5 AM	2/Lt GILBEY with two teams arrived from REGINA having been without guns and tripods were left at ZOLLERN. Position at ZERO 4 guns No 2 Section in ZOLLERN TR. 4 guns 32 MG Coy ditto. 3 guns No 1 Section in VANCOUVER TR. 1 gun No 3 Section in Strong Point at R18c 2.2 3 Guns No 3 at the BELL. 1 gun No 1 & 4 guns No 4 also at the BELL. Guns of Nos 1 & 3 sections allotted. 2 (No 1) to SUFFOLKS 1 (No 1) to NORFOLKS 1 (No 3) to ESSEX 2 (No 3) to R. BERKS	
		5.45 AM	ZERO. V Corps attacked N of ANCRE. 39th & 19th Divisions attacked S of ANCRE. 53 Inf Bde held in readiness to advance and take advantage of any success.	
			8 guns from ZOLLERN fired from 0 to +30' at 100 rounds per gun per minute on area 14 b 6.4 - 15 a 1.6 - 15 c 8.9 - 15 c 7.7.	
		9 AM	3 guns No 3 Section moved to join the BERKS & ESSEX 2 guns going forward to REGINA TR	

2449 Wt. W14957/M90 750,000 1/16 J.B.C. & A. Forms/C.2118/12.

Instructions regarding War Diaries and Intelligence Summaries are contained in F. S. Regs., Part II. and the Staff Manual respectively. Title Pages will be prepared in manuscript.

WAR DIARY
or
INTELLIGENCE SUMMARY
(Erase heading not required.)

Army Form C. 2118.

Place	Date	Hour	Summary of Events and Information	Remarks and references to Appendices
POZIERES	13/11/16	2.55 PM	Fire opened with 4 guns at 100 rounds per hour on road junction at R.10.b.2.6	
		5 PM	No 4 Section withdrawn to ALBERT.	
		6.15 PM (~~5.30~~)	Sgt CROOKES gun withdrawn from ESSEX	
"	14/11/16	–	56th Coy takes over line. 1 Section 32 M.G. Coy 1 Section (No 2) 53 M.G. Coy remain in ZOLLERN TR	
		2 AM	2 guns 2/Lt HALL withdrawn from REGINA. Struck by shell 7 casualties guns had to be abandoned.	
		7 AM	No 1 Section passed BELL relieved by 56 M.G. Coy & moved to ALBERT also one gun (No 3 Section) from Strong Point on right of REGINA	
"	"	11 AM	All company except No 2 Section & HQ, in billets in ALBERT	
& ALBERT		6 PM	HQ Coy ~~will~~ moved to be with Bde HQ at POZIERES CEMETARY	
POZIERES & ALBERT	15/11/16	–	Nothing to report. Targets in ANCRE valley kept under fire.	
	16/11/16	–	Early in the morning party under 2/Lt HALL salved two guns abandoned on the morning of the 14th.	
		10.30 AM	32nd M.G. Coy withdrawn completely from the line. Fire maintained on ANCRE VALLEY.	
	17/11/16	1 PM	No 4 Section left ALBERT and moved to ZOLLERN TR to relieve No 2 Section fire maintained at intervals during day. At night ravine in R.11.c searched	
	18/11/16	6.10 AM	Attack N of ANCRE by V Corps. S of ANCRE by. 19 Division. 18 Division (55 Bde) & 4 Canadian Division.	

2449 Wt. W14957/M90 750,000 1/16 J.B.C. & A. Forms/C.2118/12.

Army Form C. 2118.

Instructions regarding War Diaries and Intelligence Summaries are contained in F. S. Regs., Part II. and the Staff Manual respectively. Title Pages will be prepared in manuscript.

WAR DIARY
or
INTELLIGENCE SUMMARY

(Erase heading not required.)

Place	Date	Hour	Summary of Events and Information	Remarks and references to Appendices
POZIERES & ALBERT	18/11/16	6.40 AM	Guns opened on GRANDCOURT – PETIT MIRAUMONT Road 40 rounds per gun every 2 minutes till 9.10 am. The 40 rounds per gun every five minutes, continued for remainder of day	
– " –	19/11/16	–	Firing kept up steadily till midday when eased down and cleaned guns	
		9.15 AM	Company (less O.C. Company & No 4 Section with limbers) left ALBERT for CONTAY moving with whole of 53 Inf. Bde	
POZIERES & CONTAY	20/11/16	–	No 4 Section withdrawn at 9 AM. Reached ALBERT with guns & stores at 12 noon. Limbers packed & sent forward to CONTAY where remainder of company remained for the day. No 4 Section billetted in ALBERT for the night	
ALBERT & CONTAY	21/11/16	8.30	No 4 Section left ALBERT by lorry for VAL-de-MAISON. Company marched from CONTAY to VAL de MAISON.	
VAL-DE-MAISON	22/11/16	–	Entire Company rested at VAL-DE-MAISON.	
VAL-DE-MAISON	23/11/16	–	Company marched to HEM (near DOULLENS). Parade 9.45. Arrived billets 3.30 P.M. Casualties Nil. Lt WALLACE left by train from DOULLENS for final billetting area. (Route via BEAUVAL & GEZAINCOURT)	
HEM	24/11/16	–	Company marched to GRIMONT (near LE MEILLARD) Parade 9.15 AM. Arrived billets 2.45. Casualties Nil. (Route via MEZEROLLES, LE MEILLARD & HEUZECOURT)	
GRIMONT	25/11/16	–	Company marched to COULONVILLERS. Parade 9.35 AM. Arrived at billets 1 P.M. Casualties 1 (Route via PROUVILLE. DOMLÉGER. CRAMONT)	

2449 Wt. W14957/M90 750,000 1/16 J.B.C. & A. Forms/C.2118/12.

Army Form C. 2118.

Instructions regarding War Diaries and Intelligence Summaries are contained in F. S. Regs., Part II. and the Staff Manual respectively. Title Pages will be prepared in manuscript.

WAR DIARY
or
INTELLIGENCE SUMMARY

(Erase heading not required.)

Place	Date	Hour	Summary of Events and Information	Remarks and references to Appendices
~~26/11/16~~ COULONVILLERS	26/11/16	–	Company moved to FONTAINE. via FESTEL. MOULIN d'YVRENCH. YVRENCH. Inspection by G.O.C. 18 Division en route. Casualties .. Nil	
FONTAINE	27/11/16	–	Company moved to LAMOTTE-BULEUX via CANCHY. Casualties Nil	
LAMOTTE-BULEUX	28/11/16	–	Resting in billets.	
– " –	29/11/16	–	Training commenced. Preliminary work.	
– " –	30/11/16	–	Training. Practice with the Pack Saddle Equipment.	

[illegible]
Major

2449 Wt. W14957/M90 750,000 1/16 J.B.C. & A. Forms/C.2118/12.

Army Form C. 2118.

Instructions regarding War Diaries and Intelligence Summaries are contained in F. S. Regs., Part II. and the Staff Manual respectively. Title Pages will be prepared in manuscript.

WAR DIARY
or
INTELLIGENCE SUMMARY

(Erase heading not required.)

Place	Date	Hour	Summary of Events and Information	Remarks and references to Appendices

2449 Wt. W14957/M90 750,000 1/16 J.B.C. & A. Forms/C.2118/12.

Vol 10

War Diary

for month of

December 1916

for 53rd Machine Gun Company.

[signature]
Major.

Instructions regarding War Diaries and Intelligence Summaries are contained in F. S. Regs., Part II. and the Staff Manual respectively. Title Pages will be prepared in manuscript.

WAR DIARY
or
~~INTELLIGENCE SUMMARY~~

(Erase heading not required.)

Army Form C. 2118.

Place	Date	Hour	Summary of Events and Information	Remarks and references to Appendices
LAMOTTE-BULEUX	1-12-16	9am-1PM	Training Class A (recruits etc) Mechanism & Simple Tactical work Class B Tactical handling and use of ground	
–"–	2nd	–"–	Training Class A programme continued Class B Reconnaissance and use of ground	
–"–	3rd	—	Sunday	
–"–	4"	9am-1PM	Class A Passing out examination Class B Scheme for defence of village of LAMOTTE BULEUX	
–"–	5	–	Brigade Route March Machine Guns carried on pack saddles Brigade Lecture by Major J.K. DUNLOP	
–"–	6	–	Sections Parade Training Schedule	
–"–	7	– Morn Aft	Anniversary of Formation of Company. Muster Parade. 2 Sections Baths 2 sections washing limbers 2 Sections and Transport at baths	

John K Dunlop Major

2449 Wt. W14957/M90 750,000 1/16 J.B.C. & A. Forms/C.2118/12.

Army Form C. 2118.

Instructions regarding War Diaries and Intelligence Summaries are contained in F. S. Regs., Part II. and the Staff Manual respectively. Title Pages will be prepared in manuscript.

WAR DIARY
or
~~INTELLIGENCE SUMMARY~~

(Erase heading not required.)

Place	Date	Hour	Summary of Events and Information	Remarks and references to Appendices
LAMOTTE -BULEUX	8th	-	Heavy Rain Sections working [illegible] billets.	
		5.30 pm	Brigade Lecture on "Campaign in Mesopotamia" Major DAY Norfolk Regt	
	9th	-	Section working in billets. Mechanism Gun Drill and lecture by O.C. Company	
	10	-	Sunday	

John R. [illegible]
Major

2449 Wt. W14957/M90 750,000 1/16 J.B.C. & A. Forms/C.2118/12.

Army Form C. 2118.

Instructions regarding War Diaries and Intelligence Summaries are contained in F. S. Regs., Part II. and the Staff Manual respectively. Title Pages will be prepared in manuscript.

WAR DIARY
or
INTELLIGENCE SUMMARY
(Erase heading not required.)

Place	Date	Hour	Summary of Events and Information	Remarks and references to Appendices
LAMOTTE -BULEUX	11/12/16		Nos 1 & 2 Sections Revolver Practice on Range	
		9-1pm	Nos 3 & 4 Sections Siting Positions Company visited by II Corps M. G. O. Lecture by Brigade Major ESPRIT de CORPS	
	12"	–	Brigade Route March	
	13	–	Training Packing Limbers and Siting Positions	
	14"	–	Sections Training with Limbers.	
	15	–	All Sections Scheme for Defence of village from 15 16 guns	
		aft	~~Brigade Elimination Competition for Divisional Sports~~	
		Evening	Lecture by Col Park Beresford "Internal Economy"	
	16"	–	All Sections "Refresher Classes" Packing limbers Stoppages etc	
	17"	–	Sunday	[illegible] Major

2449 Wt. W14957/M90 750,000 1/16 J.B.C. & A. Forms/C.2118/12.

Army Form C. 2118.

Instructions regarding War Diaries and Intelligence Summaries are contained in F. S. Regs., Part II. and the Staff Manual respectively. Title Pages will be prepared in manuscript.

WAR DIARY
or
~~INTELLIGENCE SUMMARY~~

(Erase heading not required.)

Place	Date	Hour	Summary of Events and Information	Remarks and references to Appendices
LAMOTTE-BULEUX	18th	-	Revolver Practice on Range Brigade Gymkhana at LE TITRE	
-"-	19th	-	Brigade Route March	
-"-	20	-	Training. Two Sections attached to 8th Suffolks. 2 to Royal Berks	
-"-	21st	-	Revolver practice on R. Berks Range.	
-"-	22	-	Training Programme and baths	
-"-	23	-	Two Sections attached for training to 8th Norfolks Two to 10th Essex	
	24	-	Sunday.	

[signature]

2449 Wt. W14957/M90 750,000 1/16 J.B.C. & A. Forms/C.2118/12.

Army Form C. 2118.

Instructions regarding War Diaries and Intelligence Summaries are contained in F. S. Regs., Part II. and the Staff Manual respectively. Title Pages will be prepared in manuscript.

WAR DIARY
or
INTELLIGENCE SUMMARY
(Erase heading not required.)

Place	Date	Hour	Summary of Events and Information	Remarks and references to Appendices
LAMOTTE BULEUX	25	–	Christmas Day, Holiday & Company Dinner	
	26	–	Divisional Gymkhana	
	27	9 am – 1 PM	Tactical handling in conjunction with Infantry	
		5.30 pm	Lecture "Scouting & Reconnaissance"	
	28	9 am – 1 PM	Revolver Practice on Range	
	29	–	Company moved from LAMOTTE-BULEUX to DRUCAT. Parade 8.45 passed starting point 9.30. Route Cross Roads at NOUVILLY L'HOPITAL . PLESSIEL. Arrived billets 1 P.M. Casualties – Nil.	
	30	–	Cleaned limbers and belts. Area for training reconnoitred	
	31	–	Sunday.	

No. 53 MACHINE GUN COMPANY.
No. —
Date 7-1-17

Major

2449 Wt. W14957/M90 750,000 1/16 J.B.C. & A. Forms/C.2118/12.

Vol XI

War Diary for

January 1917.

53rd Machine Gun Company.

John K. D. [illegible] Major

Instructions regarding War Diaries and Intelligence Summaries are contained in F. S. Regs., Part II. and the Staff Manual respectively. Title Pages will be prepared in manuscript.

WAR DIARY
or
INTELLIGENCE SUMMARY
(Erase heading not required.)

Army Form C. 2118.

Place	Date	Hour	Summary of Events and Information	Remarks and references to Appendices
DRUCAT	1st	9 AM	Parade by sections. Drill order. 1 fighting limber per section. Section training in ST RIQUIER training area.	
	2nd	8.45 9 am	Parade 1 & 2 Sections. Fighting order and mule transport 3 & 4 fighting order with limbers. Nos 1 & 2 cooperating with 10 Essex in battalion scheme. 3 & 4 section training	
	3rd	–	Brigade Operations. Practice attack on MIRAUMONT on ST RIQUIER training area. No 1 Section ~~[illegible]~~ represented barrage Lt. [illegible] being chief barrage officer. No 2 Section representing defence. No 3 Section with attack on Right, No 4 on left.	
	4th	–	Section moved off to train with battalion but owing to bad weather had to return to billets	
	5th	8.45 9 am	1 & 2 Sections in fighting order with limbers 3 & 4 Section in same order. All section training in conjunction with battalions	

[illegible signature] Major

Instructions regarding War Diaries and Intelligence Summaries are contained in F. S. Regs., Part II. and the Staff Manual respectively. Title Pages will be prepared in manuscript.

WAR DIARY
or
INTELLIGENCE SUMMARY

(Erase heading not required.)

Army Form C. 2118.

Place	Date	Hour	Summary of Events and Information	Remarks and references to Appendices
DRUCAT	6th	–	Brigade Operations. Practice attack on MIRAUMONT. Barrage arrangements as for 3rd. No 3 section with defence. Nos 4 & 2 with assault. No 2 on right No 4 on left.	
	7th	–	Sunday.	
	8th	10.30am	Brigade Operation. Practice attack on a line W of MIRAUMONT. Barrage arrangements as before. No 4 section with defence. No 3 on Right with Norfolks. No 2 on left with 6 Royal Berks.	
		2.45pm	Inspection of Transport of Brigade by G.O.C. II Corps. Very wet.	
	9th	–	Very wet.	
	10	–	Preparing for move.	

[illegible signature]

2449 Wt. W14957/M90 750,000 1/16 J.B.C. & A. Forms/C.2118/12.

Instructions regarding War Diaries and Intelligence Summaries are contained in F. S. Regs., Part II. and the Staff Manual respectively. Title Pages will be prepared in manuscript.

WAR DIARY
or
INTELLIGENCE SUMMARY
(Erase heading not required.)

Army Form C. 2118.

Place	Date	Hour	Summary of Events and Information	Remarks and references to Appendices
DRUCAT	~~8am~~ 11th	8 am	Parade for move to BEAUMETZ. Move via NEUF-MOULIN ST RIQUIER COULONVILLERS. Conditions good. Casualties nil. Billeting party Lt J.O.R. Evans and 3 OR. Rear party 2/Lt W.H. HALL and 9 OR.	
		1.15pm	Reached billets.	
BEAUMETZ	12	8.30am	Paraded for move to GEZAINCOURT. Marched via (BERNAVILLE) ~~BIENVILLERS~~ HEM. Billeting party Lt J.O.R Evans and 3 O.R. Rear Party 2/Lt J.H. Caesar and 9 O.R. Conditions stormy. Casualties nil.	
GEZAINCOURT	13	–	Rested ~~that~~ day in billets in GEZAINCOURT	
– " –	14	8.50 am	Parade for move to PUCHEVILLERS. Marched via BEAUQESNE VAUCHELLES. Company under command of Lt F.G. SHOTTER. Billeting party under Lt J.O.R. Evans. Rear Party 2/Lt J.H. Caesar. & 9 O.R. O.C. Company left Bde HQ GEZAINCOURT 11 am in car for MARTINSART to discuss relief with O.C. 184 M.G. Coy. Returned direct to PUCHEVILLERS at 8 pm.	
PUCHEVILLERS	15	9 am	Parade for move to MARTINSART. Move by TOUTENCOURT - VADENCOURT - WARLOY - SENLIS - BOUZINCOURT. O.C. Coy, Lt J.O.R. Evans and 3 O.R. billeting party. Great congestion on road. Casualties nil. HQ & Transport Section billeted in MARTINSART village, section in MACKENZIE huts.	[signature]

2449 Wt. W14957/M90 750,000 1/16 J.B.C. & A. Forms/C.2118/12.

Instructions regarding War Diaries and Intelligence Summaries are contained in F. S. Regs., Part II. and the Staff Manual respectively. Title Pages will be prepared in manuscript.

WAR DIARY
or
INTELLIGENCE SUMMARY

(Erase heading not required.)

Army Form C. 2118.

Place	Date	Hour	Summary of Events and Information	Remarks and references to Appendices
MARTINSART	16th	–	Worked all day at cleaning huts in MACKENZIE hutments and in getting horse standings cleaned.	
–"–	17	–	Worked in billets.	
–"–	18th	9.30am	2 NCO's and 30 men working in THIEPVAL WOOD preparing bed for a pipe line visited by OC Coy.	
–"–	19th	9.30am	2 NCO's 30 men 1 Cook. to THIEPVAL WOOD to carry on work as above	
–"–	20th	–	2 NCO's 31 men to THIEPVAL Wood 1 officer 30 OR working under Town Major	
		10a	OC Company Lt S.R. Pocock 2/Lt W.H. HALL to MOUQUET Farm to visit sector now held by 52 Bde [illegible]	
–"–	21st	9.30am	2 NCO: 31 men to THIEPVAL Wood 1 officer 30 OR working under Town Major 1 NCO 6 O.R working under O/C baths. 2 signallers to demonstration of Fullerphone. C.S.M. to MOUQUET FARM [illegible] to reconnoitre	
		7pm	Lt J.O.R. Evans + 3 OR to MOUQUET FARM to reconnoitre	
–"–	22nd	9.30am	2 NCO. 31 men to THIEPVAL Wood 1 off 30 OR to Town Major Lt J.O.R. Evans	
		2.30pm	OC Coy. 2/Lt J.H. CAESAR, and NCOs and men from Nos 2. 3 & 4 sections to MOUQUET FARM to reconnoitre sector	
–"–	23rd	10.30	Visit by Lt/Col Brocklebank M.G.O. II Corps	
		3.30pm	Company conference Lt SHOTTER to trenches to reconnoitre	[signature] Major

2449 Wt. W14957/M90 750,000 1/16 J.B.C. & A. Forms/C.2118/12.

Army Form C. 2118.

Instructions regarding War Diaries and Intelligence Summaries are contained in F. S. Regs., Part II. and the Staff Manual respectively. Title Pages will be prepared in manuscript.

WAR DIARY
or
INTELLIGENCE SUMMARY
(Erase heading not required.)

Place	Date	Hour	Summary of Events and Information	Remarks and references to Appendices
MARTINSART	24th	9.30	1 officer 30 OR working under Town Major. Hard Frost	
— " —	25	–	1 officer 30 OR working under Town Major	
		2.30pm	Conference of C.O's and Adjutants at Bde HQ	
— " —	26	–	1 officer 30 OR working under Town Major	
			Conference at HQ 99 M.G. Coy, AVELUY of M.G. Company Commanders in II Corps called by Lt Col BROCKLEBANK M.G.O II Corps	
— " —	27	–	COMPANY relieved 54 M.G. Coy in the line. Sections passed NAB JUNCTION as follows. No 3 4.25 pm. No 1 4.45 pm. No 2 5.5 pm. No 4 5.25 pm.	
		6pm	Coy HQ established at MOUQUET FARM.	
			Disposition of guns and arrangement of company as per Appendices A & B. Relief quiet and without casualties. One LEWIS GUN team of SUFFOLKS attached as escort to No 3 gun 90.95 and 1 NCO & 8 men of NORFOLKS attached as ration carriers	
MOUQUET FARM	28		All quiet at all gun positions during day	
		6pm	Two new gun positions taken up in HESSIAN TRENCH as noted in Appendix	[signature]

2449 Wt. W14957/M90 750,000 1/16 J.B.C. & A. Forms/C.2118/12.

Instructions regarding War Diaries and Intelligence Summaries are contained in F. S. Regs., Part II. and the Staff Manual respectively. Title Pages will be prepared in manuscript.

WAR DIARY
or
INTELLIGENCE SUMMARY
(Erase heading not required.)

Army Form C. 2118.

Place	Date	Hour	Summary of Events and Information	Remarks and references to Appendices
MOUQUET FARM.	29th	–	All quiet on Company front. All guns visited by O.C. & 2nd i/c. No 10 gun fired during night on German work ~~[illegible]~~ ~~[illegible]~~ ~~[illegible]~~ in R.10.c in order to prevent them joining Coffee Tr to TEA Trench.	
– " –	30th	1.30pm	Fairly Quiet. Dug out of No 8 gun hit by a 5.9 three men buried but no one hurt. Gun undamaged	
		7.55pm	From this hour Nos 9. 10 & 11 guns fired onto R.10.c	
– " –	31st	–	Situation Quiet Casualties Nil	
		6.30	From this hour Nos 9 & 10 guns fired onto R.10.c	

[signature] Major
O.C. 53 Mg Coy

2449 Wt. W14957/M90 750,000 1/16 J.B.C. & A. Forms/C.2118/12.

AM '17

Section		Name	Post	Map reference
No 1 Section (Lt. F. G. SHOTTER)	1.	Cpl Webb.	No ~~12~~ 13	R. 21. c. 40·80
	2.	Sgt Lindopp	No ~~13~~ 14	R. 21 c. 30·80.
	3.	Sgt Burkill	No 11.	R 21 d. 10·05.
	4.	L/Cpl Robinson	– " –	– " –
No 2 Section. (Lt J. O. R. Evans)	1.	Sgt Knight	No 5 (old No 3)	R. 22 b. 90.95.
	2.	Sgt Beswick	No 6 (old No 5 & 6)	R 22 b. 40.40.
	3	Cpl Chenery	No 2 (from old No 6)	R 22 d. 80.80
	4	L/Cpl Scott	No 3	R 23 b. 15.10
No ~~2~~ 4 Section. (2/Lt W. H. HALL)	1.	Cpl Walton	No 8	R 22 a 60.70
	2.	Cpl Hall	No 9 }	R 22 c 15·40
	3	Sgt Tuly	No 10 }	
	4.	Sgt Rogers	No 12.	R 21 d 20·80.
No 3 Section (2/Lt J. H Caesar M.C.)	1	Sgt Silverwood	No 1	R 23. b 25·15
	2	Sgt Crookes	No 4	R 22 d 70.70
	3	L/Cpl Norris }	Mouquet Farm.	
	4	Pte Philips. }		

John ... Major

GRANDCOURT
GRANDCOURT TRENCH
BATTERY VALLEY
DESIRE TRENCH
STUMP ROAD
GRANDCOURT ROAD
SIXTEEN ROAD
REGINA TRENCH
SECOND
ASSEMBLY TRENCH
HESSIAN TRENCH
STUFF REDOUBT
BAINBRIDGE TRENCH
ZOLLERN REDOUBT
FIELD TRENCH
ZOLLERN TRENCH EAST
COURCELETTE
FABRIC TRENCH
HIGH TRENCH
MOUQUET FARM

War Diary

for

53 L.T.G. Coy

for

February 1917

Vol 12

Instructions regarding War Diaries and Intelligence Summaries are contained in F. S. Regs., Part II. and the Staff Manual respectively. Title pages will be prepared in manuscript.

WAR DIARY
or
INTELLIGENCE SUMMARY.
(Erase heading not required.)

Army Form C. 2118.

Place	Date	Hour	Summary of Events and Information	Remarks and references to Appendices
MOUQUET FARM	1st 7 Feb	–	Company in the line, guns in positions as per attached map appendix A. No 9 & 10 guns fired at night on COFFEE TRENCH. Visibility bad. No enemy movement observed	'A' positions underlined marked 1st Position
– " –	2nd	–		
– " –	3rd	–	Situation quiet during day – In connection with attack by 63 (RN) Division on N of River ANCRE, Nos 9 & 10 guns fired on line R 4 d. 4 4 to R 10 b. 0 8	
		11.30 pm	also line R 4 c 4 4 to R 10 a 4 4 intensely till 1.30 am	
– " –	4	1.30 am	Rate of fire of Nos 9 & 10 decreased to intermittent firing till dawn. Expenditure 10.500 rounds	
		10.30 am	No 9 & 10 reopened in reply to SOS from 63 Division, also shortly afterwards Nos 3 & 4 over a line N & S through Mill. Rate of fire one belt per gun per 5 minutes	
		12.30 pm	Ceased fire, refilled belts, & stood down	
– " –		8 pm till midnight	Alternate firing on barrage lines carried on all night by No 4 section (2/Lt HALL) & No 3 Section (2/Lt Caesar) except from 12.30 am till 1.40 a (5 minutes)	

A5834 Wt. W4973/M687 750,000 8/16 D. D. & L. Ltd. Forms/C.2118/13.

Army Form C. 2118.

Instructions regarding War Diaries and Intelligence Summaries are contained in F. S. Regs., Part II. and the Staff Manual respectively. Title pages will be prepared in manuscript.

WAR DIARY
or
INTELLIGENCE SUMMARY.
(Erase heading not required.)

Place	Date	Hour	Summary of Events and Information	Remarks and references to Appendices
MOUQUET FARM	5th	1 am	ESSEX raided FOLLY TR.	
		1.20 am	Nos 9 & 10 (2/Lt HALL) fired on line 6°–7° Rt elevation +6°–8°. Rate of fire 12 belts per gun per hour. (area fired on R.10 central)	
		1.40 am	Ceased fire	
		–	During morning MOUQUET FARM was shelled with 5.9's. About 20 rounds, one every quarter of an hour.	
		7 pm onwards	Nos 9 & 10 guns fired on GRANDCOURT – MIRAUMONT road	
			During night 5/6 63 (RN) Division occupied without opposition OG 1 & OG 2	
	6th	–	Quiet Day with little visibility	
		7.30 pm	In response to orders from Brigade to harassed all routes by which enemy might withdraw Nos 9 & 10 3 & 4 fired ~~placed~~ barrage across line of railway & MIRAUMONT – GRANDCOURT ROAD (3 & 4 4° Lft bracket 8° to 11° elevation 9 & 10 8° Rt bracket 7°27' to 11°)	
	7th	2.45 am	ESSEX occupied R15c 70 & 21 without opposition. Sgt BURKILL'S team moved to No 9 & 10 to assist teams there in beltfilling.	
			Day Quiet. Enemy's shelling light. Visibility fair	
			~~Night Nos 9 & 10 guns fired on GRANDCOURT – MIRAUMONT Road. Expenditure [illegible] rounds~~	

A5834 Wt. W4973/M687 750,000 8/16 D. D. & L. Ltd. Forms/C.2118/13.

Instructions regarding War Diaries and Intelligence Summaries are contained in F. S. Regs., Part II. and the Staff Manual respectively. Title pages will be prepared in manuscript.

WAR DIARY
or
INTELLIGENCE SUMMARY.
(Erase heading not required.)

Army Form C. 2118.

Place	Date	Hour	Summary of Events and Information	Remarks and references to Appendices
MOUQUET FARM	7th Oct	1pm	OC Coy ordered to Conference at Bde HQ.	
		3.pm	OC Coy reconnoitred with Sgt ROBERTS position for guns in STUMP ROAD	
		4.30pm	Conference at Coy HQ. MAJOR HEYLAND 55 M.G. Coy present	
		–	Sgt LINDOP & Cpl WEBB: guns (No 1 Section) ordered to report to Capt THOMPSON D Coy ~~...~~ ESSEX. to move with them to GUNPITS	
		6.50pm	Orders issued for disposition of guns available as follows.	
			(a) Sgt BURKILL. Sgt ROBERTS. Cpl WALTON. Sgt TOBY under Lt EVANS & 2/Lt HALL to move to STUMP ROAD	
			(b) 4 guns 55 Coy to move to STUMP ROAD	
			(c) 4 guns 55 at Nos 9 & 10 position	
			(d) 2 guns. REGINA TR. Nos 8 & 8A (Cpl HALL & Sgt BESWICK) under 2/Lt BROWN	
			(e) 2 guns Sgt LINDOP. Cpl WEBB as above	
			(f) Advanced HQ at No 12 position	
			(g) ~~...~~ No 1. 2 ~~gun~~ moved ~~unchanged~~ / to Nos 3 & 4	
			(h) Sgt KNIGHT not moved	
		11pm	Everything ready.	
	8	1.30am	ZERO Combined ~~...~~ firing, by guns of both companies	
		5.15 am	Fire ceased from STUMP ROAD. 55 Company withdrawn	
		5.20	All guns from STUMP ROAD except Sgt BURKILL ~~...~~ returned to original position with the exception of ~~that~~ of Sgt BURKILL.	[signature]

A5834 Wt. W4973/M687 750,000 8/16 D. D. & L. Ltd. Forms/C.2118/13.

Instructions regarding War Diaries and Intelligence Summaries are contained in F. S. Regs., Part II. and the Staff Manual respectively. Title pages will be prepared in manuscript.

WAR DIARY
or
INTELLIGENCE SUMMARY.
(Erase heading not required.)

Army Form C. 2118.

Place	Date	Hour	Summary of Events and Information	Remarks and references to Appendices
MOUQUET FARM	8th	6am	No 8 guns ceased fire.	
			2 sections of 53 M.G. Coy went back to HEDAUVILLE	
			Quiet Day	
		6pm	Cpl CHENERY's team (No 3) moved forward to Lt EVANS	
		8.25pm	Sgt ROGERS team relieved Sgt BURKILL at STUMP Rd	
	9th	–	Quiet Day	
		–	Evening. Relief of Company by 54th M.G. Company	
–		11.30pm	Relief complete. Sections marched to MARTINSART	
MARTINSART	10th	–	Company marched to billets in HEDAUVILLE	
HEDAUVILLE	11th	–	Resting in billets cleaning guns	

A5834 Wt. W4973/M687 750,000 8/16 D. D. & L. Ltd. Forms/C.2118/13.

Instructions regarding War Diaries and Intelligence Summaries are contained in F. S. Regs., Part II. and the Staff Manual respectively. Title pages will be prepared in manuscript.

WAR DIARY
or
INTELLIGENCE SUMMARY.
(*Erase heading not required.*)

Army Form C. 2118.

Place	Date	Hour	Summary of Events and Information	Remarks and references to Appendices
HEDAUVILLE.	12	11–12.30	Section Parades for inspection. Reconnaissance of ground N of ANCRE (BEAUCOURT. RIVER Tr & PUISIEUX TR) by O.C. Coy & 2/Lt CAESAR	
– " –	13.	9.30 am	Company paraded for short route march. Company bathed.	
– " –	14	9.30	Company paraded as above.	
		11.30	O.C. Coy 2/Lt CAESAR. Sgt MILLER & Sgt CROOKES met at NAB JUNCTION & reconnoitred ~~ground~~ ~~to~~ ~~ga~~ STUMP ROAD & GRANDCOURT scheme via St. PIERRE DIVION.	
– " –	15	1.pm	Company moved to Line Nos 1 & 3 Sections paraded to move off.	
		1.15 pm	Nos 2 & 4 " " " Disposition of company as per attached plan	'B'
		7.30 pm	Relief complete	
	16	–	All guns of No 2 Section concentrated in dugout near junction of STUMP ROAD & LUCKY WAY. And ammunition taken up to gun positions. Day spent in preparation of minor arrangements	

A5834 Wt. W4973/M687 750,000 8/16 D. D. & L. Ltd. Forms/C.2118/13.

Instructions regarding War Diaries and Intelligence Summaries are contained in F. S. Regs., Part II. and the Staff Manual respectively. Title pages will be prepared in manuscript.

WAR DIARY
or
INTELLIGENCE SUMMARY.
(*Erase heading not required.*)

Army Form C. 2118.

Place	Date	Hour	Summary of Events and Information	Remarks and references to Appendices
ZOLLERN TRENCH	17th	2am	1 Gun No1 Section (L/Cpl GEE) under 2/Lt BROWN reached point at R.16 d. 5.9.	
		5.15 am	Zero. Position of Company. 2 Sections Nos 2 & 3 STUMP ROAD & GUN PITS. 1 Section No1. ready to move forward. 1 Section No 6 Reserve.	
			Nos 2 & 3 Sections opened fire at ZERO in accordance with II Corps programme. In addition 8 guns 54 MG Coy fired from O.G.1. & 4 guns 55 MG Coy from LUCKY WAY	
		10.15	2 guns from reserve Sgt JUBY Cpl WALTON ordered to report OC 6 Royal BERKS.	
		10.30 am	2/Lt BROWN ordered forward to GRANDCOURT TR.	
		10.30 am	3 gun teams No1 Section moved forward from HESSIAN & REGINA trenches with parties of RE to strong points. Sgt BURKILL to position on RAILWAY Sgt LINDOP to R.10 b 3.3 Cpl WEBB to R.10 a 3.7	
		Noon	2/Lt BROWN established at R.16 b. 8.9 covering the flank of Brigade left open by count attacks on 2 Division	
		1pm	Sgt JUBY reached position just forward of TEA TR R.10 a 5.5 20. Cpl WALTON on road at R.10 a 30.35	
		–	One gun on STUMP ROAD knocked out by shrapnel	
		–	Gun in GRANDCOURT TR shelled out of position moved to R.16 b. 6.8	
		–	Night Quiet	[signature]

A5834 Wt. W4973/M687 750,000 8/16 D. D. & L. Ltd. Forms/C.2118/13.

Army Form C. 2118.

Instructions regarding War Diaries and Intelligence Summaries are contained in F. S. Regs., Part II. and the Staff Manual respectively. Title pages will be prepared in manuscript.

WAR DIARY
or
INTELLIGENCE SUMMARY.
(Erase heading not required.)

Place	Date	Hour	Summary of Events and Information	Remarks and references to Appendices
ZOLLERN TR	18th	DAWN	Party of about 75 enemy caught by Sgt TUBY trying to withdraw from R10C 2.9 in the mist. Many hit.	
		–	Throughout the day guns in STUMP ROAD fired on areas N of Mill & Grand in R5A	
		–	New position sited in RUM TR. about pt 9.2	
		Evening	2 teams No 3 Section relieved Sgt LINDOP & Cpl WEBB	
	19th	DAWN	Sgt ROBERTS relieved Sgt BURKILL gun Railway. Sgt TUBY & Cpl WALTON withdrawn. Cpl HALL (No 4) occupied new position. 2/Lt W.H. HALL sniped through the heat in front of TEA TR. 55th M.G. Coy took over L/Cpl GEE's position in GRANDCOURT TR.	
	20th	–	55 M.G. Coy moved out of LUCKY WAY gun positions. These occupied by 3 guns No 2 Section & 2 guns No 3.	
	21.	–	Sgt Burkill & Sgt LINDOP (No 1) relieved Sgt Crocker & L/Cpl Scott (No 3)	
	22.	–	Sgt Lindop's gun R10C 3.3 withdrawn	
	23	–	Responsibility for line taken over by 55 M.G. Coy. All 53 M.G. Coy withdrawn with exception of 2 guns (No 2) & 1 gun (No 3) under Lt EVANS at LUCKY WAY	

A5834 Wt. W4973/M687 750,000 8/16 D. D. & L. Ltd. Forms/C.2118/13.

GRANDCOURT
GRANDCOURT TRENCH
DESIRE TRENCH
STUMP ROAD
REGINA TRENCH
SECOND
ASSEMBLY TRENCH
HESSIAN TRENCH
HESSIAN
TIRTOR REDOUBT
BAINBRIDGE TRENCH
Zollern Redoubt
FIELD TRENCH
SIXTEEN ROAD
GRANDCOURT Rd.
REGINA
ZOLLERN
TRENCH EAST.
COURCELETTE
FABRIC TRENCH
HIGH TRENCH
MOUQUET FARM.
BATTERY VALLEY
R
18
12
11
17
16
15
24
23
22
21
20
26
27
28
29
30

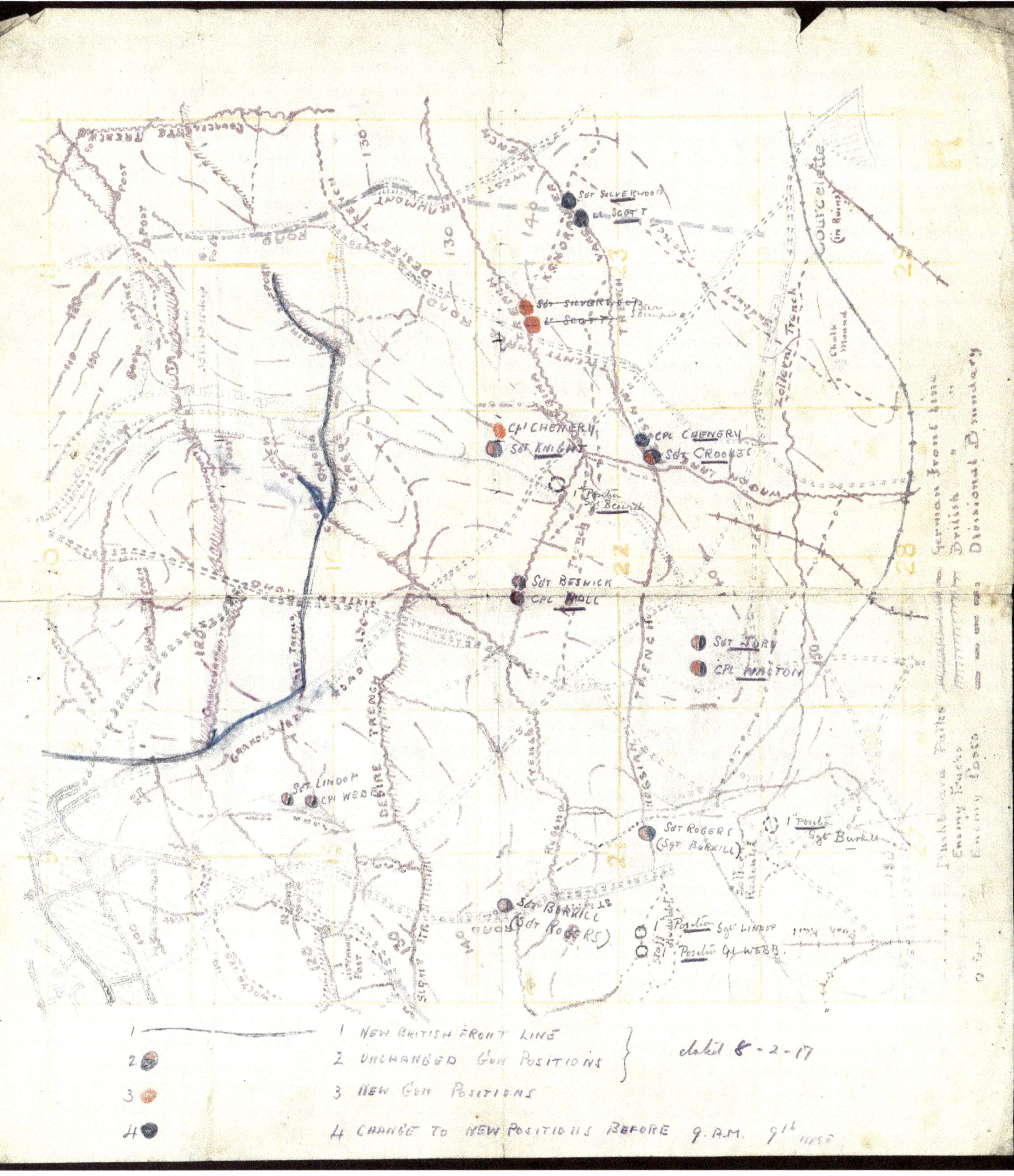

Sgt Silverwood
Lt Scott
Cpl Chenery
Sgt Knight
Cpl Chenery
Sgt Crooks
1st Position Sgt Beswick
Sgt Beswick
Cpl Hall
Sgt Jury
Cpl Walton
Sgt Lindop
Cpl Webb
Sgt Rogers (Sgt Burkill)
1st Position Sgt Burkill
Sgt Burkill (Sgt Rogers)
1st Position Sgt Lindop
2nd Position Cpl Webb
Courcelette (in Ruins)
Zollern Trench
Chalk Mound
Desire Trench
Hessian Trench
Grandcourt Road
German Front Line
British "
Divisional Boundary
1 New British Front Line
2 Unchanged Gun Positions
3 New Gun Positions
4 Change to new positions before 9.A.M. 9th inst
dated 8-2-17

APPENDIX J2

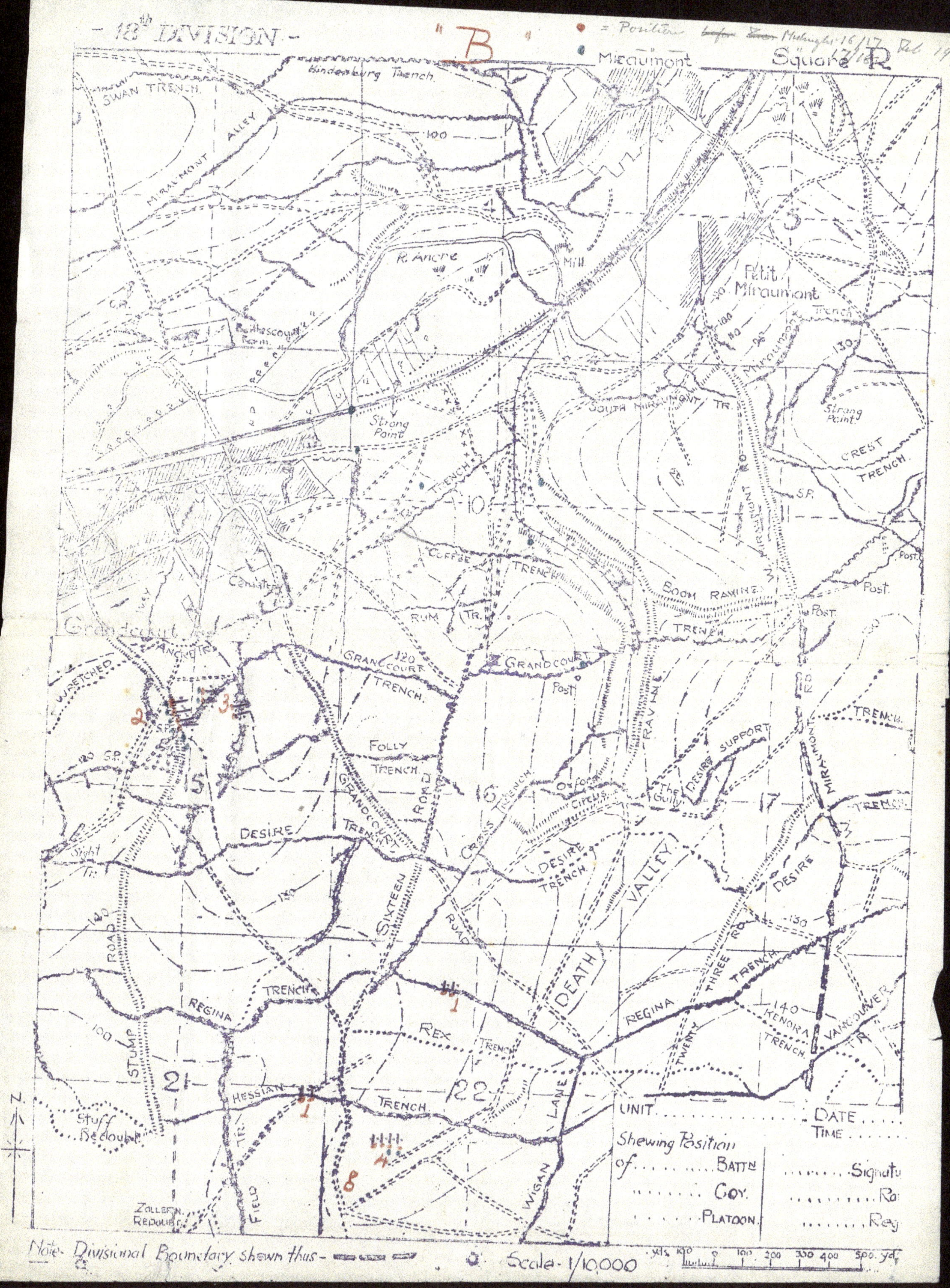

18th DIVISION
"B"
= Position
Midnight 16/17 Feb 1917
Miraumont
Square R
Hindenburg Trench
SWAN TRENCH
MIRAUMONT ALLEY
R. Ancre
Mill
Petit Miraumont
SOUTH MIRAUMONT TR.
Strong Point
CREST TRENCH
COFFEE TRENCH
BOOM RAVINE
RUM TR.
GRANDCOURT TRENCH
FOLLY TRENCH
DESIRE SUPPORT
The Gully
DESIRE TRENCH
DEATH VALLEY
SIXTEEN ROAD
REGINA TRENCH
REX TRENCH
HESSIAN TRENCH
KENORA TRENCH
VANCOUVER TR.
WIGAN LANE
STUMP ROAD
Stuff Redoubt
ZOLLERN REDOUBT
FIELD TR.
UNIT .... DATE ......
TIME ......
Shewing Position of .... BATTN .... Signature
.... COY. .... Rank
.... PLATOON. .... Regt
Note- Divisional Boundary shewn thus-
Scale- 1/10,000

APPENDIX B

Vol 13

War Diary

for March 1917

of

53rd M. G. Coy.

[illegible] Major

Instructions regarding War Diaries and Intelligence Summaries are contained in F. S. Regs., Part II. and the Staff Manual respectively. Title pages will be prepared in manuscript.

WAR DIARY
or
INTELLIGENCE SUMMARY.
(Erase heading not required.)

Army Form C. 2118.

Place	Date	Hour	Summary of Events and Information	Remarks and references to Appendices
~~MARLBOROUGH~~ MACKENZIE HUTS (AVELUY)	1 March	9-30 am	Company parade followed by gas helmet drill. Roads to PETIT MIRAUMONT. the village & 130 contour reconnoitred by OC by. Lt EVANS Lt WALLACE & Lt POCOCK	
	2 " "	9.30 am	Company parade. Further reconnaisance.	
	3 " "	11am	Company moved to MARLBOROUGH HUTS.	
		1pm	Company clear of Mackenzie Huts. Transport lines at QM Stores established E. of NAB VALLEY ROAD opposite MARLBOROUGH HUTS. - 2/LIEUT BROWN evacuated sick	
		3.45 pm	Sections left MALBOROUGH HUTS to relieve 55 M.G. Coy moving by duck-boards via RIFLE DUMP. Transport moved via HAMEL. STPIERRE DIVION and GRANDCOURT. Company rendezvoused at R.10.b.2.6	
		9. pm	Relief complete	
			Position of Company. Coy HQ R10d also 4 guns. 2 guns with officer L 30.a.2.0. 1 gun L 35 5 guns with officer ~~M~~ & E. MIRAUMONT ROAD in R.11.b 2 guns with officer at M.2.a.1.4. 2 guns reserve at R.22.b.90.95.	[illegible]
	4 " "	-	Positions visited. Situation Quiet	
			Two gun teams No2 section moved from R.22.b 90.95 to dugout at SIXTEEN ROAD	
		11pm	Warning order received that enemy had been seen possibly concentrating at G.20.c. Lt COATES with party of ESSEX took 10.000 rounds SAA to GOODS STATION. Sgt KNIGHT's gun & team moved from reserve to position at QUARRY L.35.d.	
	5 " "	DAWN	Sgt KNIGHTS team withdrawn.	
		NOON	Company HQ moved to dugout in PETIT MIRAUMONT on E. MIRAUMONT ROAD	
		2.30 pm	Reserve team of No1 Section (Lt COATES) moved up to GOODS STATION. Gun & team of Cpl WEBB (No1 SECTION) detailed to move forward in conjunction with 8' Suffolks	[signature] Capt

A5834 Wt. W4973/M687 750,000 8/16 D. D. & L. Ltd. Forms/C.2118/13.

Instructions regarding War Diaries and Intelligence Summaries are contained in F. S. Regs., Part II. and the Staff Manual respectively. Title pages will be prepared in manuscript.

Army Form C. 2118.

WAR DIARY
or
INTELLIGENCE SUMMARY.
(Erase heading not required.)

Place	Date	Hour	Summary of Events and Information	Remarks and references to Appendices
PETIT MIRAUMONT	6th	12.15 a	8 Suffolks attacked and captured RESURRECTION TR from junction with DITCH to about G25.d.21. 3 guns No 3 Section (2/Lt CAESAR) and 2 guns No 4 section (Sgt JUBY) fired at (a) QUARRY in G26.c (b) CEMETARY (c) QUARRY in G26.d and (d) QUARRY in G.32.a from ZERO till dawn. Expenditure 10.500 rounds	
			1 gun & team Cpl WEBB moved to RESURRECTION TR and were established about point G.31.a.2.9.	
		11 am – NOON	Belts all refilled and ammunition supply made up. (Coy ammunition dump at R.5.c.8.8.)	
		2.12 p – 5 pm	Area round Coy HQ R.5.a.1.2 shelled steadily at first then heavily.	
–"–	7th	10 AM	Day fairly Quiet. Party of enemy seen from GOODS STATION to be moving S of ACHIET le PETIT. Dispersed by MG Fire.	
		3.30 p	OC Visited 99 MG Coy at R.29 central	
–"–	8th		Quiet day. No changes in dispositions	
		4 pm	OC Visited MG Coy attached to 197 Brigade at R.3.c.4.4	
		5.30 pm	Area round Coy HQ shelled. Counter battery work asked for & effective	[signature] Maj

A5834 Wt. W4973/M687 750,000 8/16 D. D. & L. Ltd. Forms/C.2118/13.

Army Form C. 2118.

Instructions regarding War Diaries and Intelligence Summaries are contained in F. S. Regs., Part II. and the Staff Manual respectively. Title pages will be prepared in manuscript.

WAR DIARY
or
INTELLIGENCE SUMMARY.

(Erase heading not required.)

Place	Date	Hour	Summary of Events and Information	Remarks and references to Appendices
PETIT MIRAUMONT	~~[illegible]~~ 9	3.15 am	Guns at GOODS STATION fired in connection with bombing attack by ESSEX on point G 25 a 2 6.	
		4-5.15	GOODS STATION shelled fairly heavily.	
		10 am	Sgt JUBY commenced to establish two guns from EMIRAUMONT ROAD at M1 a [illegible] 0. These guns ready by dusk.	
		4.30pm	16 men SUFFOLK Regt reported for assistance in ration carrying.	
		5pm	Two Company cooks moved up from BOOM RAVINE to take charge of SAA dump. Sgt Silverwoods team (No 3 Section) moved from SIXTEEN ROAD to join remainder of ~~camp~~ section on EMIRAUMONT ROAD.	
		EVENING.	4 gun team No 2 Section moved from SIXTEEN Road to assembly positions	

[illegible signature]
Major

A5834 Wt. W4973/M687 750,000 8/16 D. D. & L. Ltd. Forms/C.2118/13.

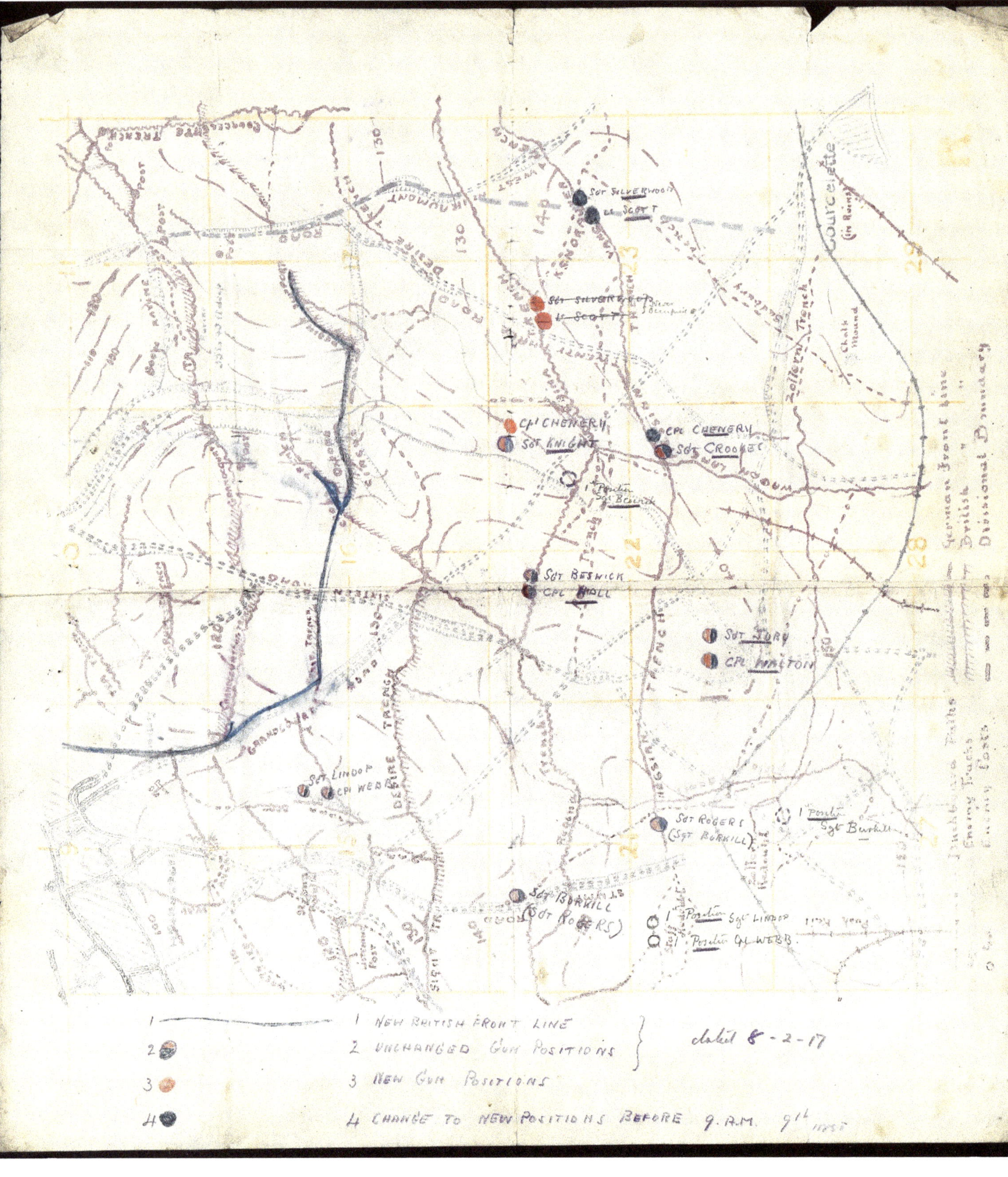

1 NEW BRITISH FRONT LINE
2 UNCHANGED GUN POSITIONS
3 NEW GUN POSITIONS
4 CHANGE TO NEW POSITIONS BEFORE 9.A.M. 9th inst
dated 8-2-17
German Front Line
British
Divisional Boundary
Duckboard Paths
Enemy Tracks
Enemy Posts
Courcelette (in Ruins)
Chalk Mound
Zollern Trench
Desire Trench
Regina Trench
Hessian Trench
Courcelette Trench
Wagon Road
Grandcourt Road
Sixteen Road
Sgt Silverwood
Lt Scott
Cpl Chenery
Sgt Knight
Cpl Chenery
Sgt Crooket
Sgt Beswick
Cpl Noll
Sgt Jory
Cpl Walton
Sgt Lindop
Cpl Webb
Sgt Rogers (Sgt Burkill)
1 Position Sgt Burkill
Sgt Burkill (Sgt Rogers)
1 Position Sgt Lindop
1 Position Cpl Webb

APPENDIX ✓Z

- 18th DIVISION -
"B"
= Position Midnight 16/17 Feb 1917
— " — 17/18
Miraumont
Square R
Hindenburg Trench
SWAN TRENCH
MIRALMONT ALLEY
R. Ancre
Mill
Petit Miraumont
Baillescourt Farm
Strong Point
SOUTH MIRAUMONT TR.
CREST TRENCH
COFFEE TRENCH
RUM TR.
BOOM RAVINE
Cemetery
Grandcourt
ANCRE TR.
WRETCHED
GRANDCOURT TRENCH
GRANDCOURT Post
FOLLY TRENCH
ROAD
CROSS TRENCH
Oxford Circus
The Gully
DESIRE SUPPORT
DESIRE TRENCH
GRANDCOURT TRENCH
Sight Tr.
SIXTEEN ROAD
DEATH VALLEY
TWENTY THREE RD
MIRAUMONT
REGINA TRENCH
REX TRENCH
KENORA TRENCH
VANCOUVER TR.
STUMP ROAD
HESSIAN TRENCH
Stuff Redoubt
ZOLLERN REDOUBT
FIELD TR.
WIGAN LANE
UNIT
DATE
TIME
Shewing Position of
BATTN
COY.
PLATOON
Signature
Rank
Regt
Note- Divisional Boundary shewn thus -
Scale - 1/10,000

Army Form C. 2118.

Instructions regarding War Diaries and Intelligence Summaries are contained in F. S. Regs., Part II. and the Staff Manual respectively. Title pages will be prepared in manuscript.

WAR DIARY
or
INTELLIGENCE SUMMARY.
(Erase heading not required.)

Place	Date	Hour	Summary of Events and Information	Remarks and references to Appendices
MARLBOROUGH HUTS	15	–	Cleaning up	
	16	9.30am – 10.30am	Parade under C.S.M. Dickinson for Drill	
	17	9.30am – 10.30am	Company parade under C.S.M. Dickinson No 3 Section detached for anti aircraft duties in AVELUY WOOD	
	18	–	Resting in billets	
	19	–	Resting in billets	

[signature] Major

A5834 Wt. W4973/M687 750,000 8/16 D. D. & L. Ltd. Forms/C.2118/13

Instructions regarding War Diaries and Intelligence Summaries are contained in F. S. Regs., Part II. and the Staff Manual respectively. Title pages will be prepared in manuscript.

WAR DIARY
or
INTELLIGENCE SUMMARY.
(Erase heading not required.)

Army Form C. 2118.

Place	Date	Hour	Summary of Events and Information	Remarks and references to Appendices
MARLBOROUGH HUTS	20th	–	Company marched to WARLOY arrived at billets 4.45 pm. No 3 Section relieved from A A duties reached WARLOY 7.30 pm. Casualties on march nil	
WARLOY.	21st	–	Resting in billets. Pay parade 2. pm	
– " –	22nd	9.15 am	Parade for march route. route WARDANCOURT. - BEAUCOURT SUR L'HALLUE. - MOLLIENS au BOIS arrived at billets 1.30 pm. Casualties on march nil.	
MOLLIENS-AU-BOIS	23rd	9.15 am	Parade for march to point on main road N end of VILLERS-BOCAGE where company entrained on 'busses and proceeded via POULAINVILLE - AMIENS - SALEUX to REVELLES arrived at REVELLES 4.45 pm having been delayed at start. Transport proceeded independently via BERTANGLES ST SAUVEUR & AILLY-SUR-SOMME to REVELLES arriving about 5.30 pm	
REVELLES	24th	–	Approaches to BACOUEL Station reconnoitred by T.O. & C.O.	
		12.30 pm	Transport left REVELLES for BACOUEL Station arrived 2 pm.	
		2.45 pm	Company left REVELLES " " " 4 pm.	
			Train badly delayed by accident. Coy bivouaced in woods N of Station	
		9.15 pm	Entrained.	
		11 PM	CHANGE TO SUMMER TIME	
IN TRAIN	25	–	Breakfast at ABBEVILLE. Route ABBEVILLE. BOULOGNE ST OMER HAZEBROUK BERGUETTE	
	26	1 AM	Detrained at BERGUETTE. bivouaced till 6.30 pm. Everyone billetted by 7 am.	
			Rested in billets during day.	
BERGUETTE	27			[signature] Maj

A5834 Wt. W4973/M687 750,000 8/16 D. D. & L. Ltd. Forms/C.2118/13.

Army Form C. 2118.

Instructions regarding War Diaries and Intelligence Summaries are contained in F. S. Regs., Part II. and the Staff Manual respectively. Title pages will be prepared in manuscript.

WAR DIARY
or
INTELLIGENCE SUMMARY.

(Erase heading not required.)

Place	Date	Hour	Summary of Events and Information	Remarks and references to Appendices
BERGUETTE	27	9.30	Coy parade under C.S.M. Dickinson	
		10.30 / 11–1	Cleaning sorting and inspection of section equipment.	
	28"	9.30 / 10.30	Coy parade under C.S.M. Dickinson.	
		11–1	Gas helmet instruction.	
	29"	9.30 / 10.30	Parade under OC Coy	
		11–1	Cleaning & refilling belts. also range finding class	
	30"	9.30	Parade under O.C. Coy.	
		10.30	Physical Drill	
		11.30	Training in Box Respirators	
		2–3.30	Stoppages & Mechanism.	
	31	9.0	Parade under O.C. Coy	
		10.30	Physical Training	
		11.30	Gun Drill Football in afternoon	[signature] Capt

A5834 Wt. W4973/M687 750,000 8/16 D. D. & L. Ltd. Forms/C.2118/13

Vol 14

War Diary for

53rd Machine Gun Company

April 1917

Ref. HAZEBROUCK (5A) 1/100.000

Instructions regarding War Diaries and Intelligence Summaries are contained in F. S. Regs., Part II. and the Staff Manual respectively. Title pages will be prepared in manuscript.

WAR DIARY 53 M.G. Coy

or

~~INTELLIGENCE SUMMARY.~~

(Erase heading not required.)

Army Form C. 2118.

1

Place	Date	Hour	Summary of Events and Information	Remarks and references to Appendices
BERGUETTE PAS-DE-CALAIS	1st 1/4/17	–	Sunday Divine Service & billet inspection	
– " –	2/4/17	–	Training	
		2.30pm	G.O.C. Brigade inspected transport of company.	
			Following published as Honours & Awards	
			Lt EVANS Military Cross	
			Sgt BESWICK D.C.M. both for gallantry at the capture of IRLES 10/3/17	
– " –	3/4/17	–	Training.	
– " –	4/4/17	–	Training. Firing on Range & tactical handling	
– " –	5/4/17	–	Brigade Concentration Route March.	
– " –	6/4/17	–	Training. Tactical handling	
		5pm	Lecture in schoolroom by Divisional Gas Officer	
			Brigade Eliminating Competition Cookers & Water Carts. First prize for water carts 53 MG C	
– " –	7/4/17	–	Sunday Church Parade of 53 & 54 Brigades (400 men per Bn) at ISEGHEM G.O.C. II Corps presented Medal Ribbons to 5 N.C.O.s & men of the company	
– " –	8/4/17	–	Training	
			AFTERNOON Divisional Transport Competition at Aire ~~[illegible]~~ 53 MG Cy took first prize for L.G.S. waggons	

A5834 Wt. W4973/M687 750,000 8/16 D. D. & L. Ltd. Forms/C.2118/13.

Ref 'HAZEBROUCK (5A) 1/100,000

Instructions regarding War Diaries and Intelligence Summaries are contained in F. S. Regs., Part II. and the Staff Manual respectively. Title pages will be prepared in manuscript.

WAR DIARY

or

~~INTELLIGENCE SUMMARY.~~

(Erase heading not required.)

53rd M.G. Coy

Army Form C. 2118.

2

Place	Date	Hour	Summary of Events and Information	Remarks and references to Appendices
BERGUETTE PAS-de-CALAIS	10/4/17	–	Training	
		10 am	Gas cloud demonstration by Divisional Gas Officer	
– " –	11/4/17	–	Training. Company route march with Advance Guard Scheme.	
– " –	12/4/17	10.30 am	G.O.C. 53rd Inf. Bde inspected Company.	
– " –	13/4/17	–	Training.	
– " –	14/4/17	–	Training. Company working as portion of ~~an~~ advance guard.	
– " –	15/4/17	–	Sunday.	
– " –	16/4/17	–	Brigade Route March. Company ordered to relieve 6 guns Divisional M.G. by 46 Division employed on A.A. Duty at TREZENNES DUMP & road ST. VENANT. ROBECQ. Position reconnoitred by O.C. Company 2/Lt LEITH & COATES.	
– " –	17/4/17	—	Scheme arranged with II Corps Cyclist Bn cancelled owing to bad weather	
		10.50 am	Relief of 46 Divisional by complete No 2 Section at ROBECQ 2/Lt LEITH No 4 – " – at TREZENNES 2/Lt ALLEN	
– " –	18/4/17	–	Training.	
BERGUETTE – BETHUNE	19/4/17	–	~~Brigade~~ moved to BETHUNE Area. Nos 2 & ½ 4 Sections were relieved by 10 am by 54 M.G. Company & moved independently to BETHUNE Company all in by 5 pm H.Q. 32 RUE DE LILLE	
	20/4/17	–	Inspection of Guns etc	

A5834 Wt. W4973/M687 750,000 8/16 D. D. & L. Ltd. Forms/C.2118/13.

LENS 11 1/100.000
51.B. 1/40.000

Instructions regarding War Diaries and Intelligence Summaries are contained in F. S. Regs., Part II. and the Staff Manual respectively. Title pages will be prepared in manuscript.

WAR DIARY

or

~~INTELLIGENCE SUMMARY.~~

(Erase heading not required.)

53rd M.G. Coy

Army Form C. 2118.

3

Place	Date	Hour	Summary of Events and Information	Remarks and references to Appendices
BETHUNE - NOEUX-les MINES	21/4/17	–	Brigade moved to area NOEUX-les MINES. Coy HQ. RUE HINGETTE	
NOEUX-les MINES.	22/4/17	–	Bde Reconnaissance of Part of Reserve ~~Support~~ line on I Corps front. OC company, Lt WALLACE, Lt SHOTTER Lt COMTET, 2/Lt CAESAR 2/Lt LEITH reconnoitred Defences of MAROC & "VILLAGE LINE"	
– " –	23/4/17	–	Reconnaissance as above carried out by Officers & NCO's of 1 & 4 Sections	
– " –	24/4/17	–	Training Reconnaissance as above carried out by Officers & NCO's of 2 & 3 Sections	
– " –	25/4/17	–	Training No 3 Section training with 10 ESSEX (Major Dinley accompanied Major Sandilands G.S.O.2 I Corps in reconnaissance of proposed reg. positions on Reserve line ANGRES to MAROC)	
– " –	26/4/17	–	Packed up & stood by ready to move	
VALHUON	27/4/17	–	Brigade marched to VALHUON. Parade 8.40 am route BARLIN - HOUDAIN - DIVION - DIEVAL - BOURS came under orders of VII Corps Third Army.	
		3.35 pm	Company arrived at billets VALHUON. Casualties on march nil	
– " –	28/4/17	–	Rested at VALHUON	
VALHUON & BEAURAINS	29/4/17	5 am	Company (less transport) moved to PERNET. CAMBLAIN Station. Entrained at 6.50 am ~~Travel~~ By train via St POL - AUBIGNY to ARRAS. Marched to bivouac position in M.10 d (BEURAINS). Transport moved via TINQUES & CHELERS to HABARQ where it rested for the night	

A5834 Wt. W4973/M687 750,000 8/16 D. D. & L. Ltd. Forms/C.2118/13.

Ref. Sheet 51.B.S.W. 4a 1/20.000.

Instructions regarding War Diaries and Intelligence Summaries are contained in F. S. Regs., Part II. and the Staff Manual respectively. Title pages will be prepared in manuscript.

WAR DIARY
or
~~INTELLIGENCE SUMMARY.~~
(Erase heading not required.)

Army Form C. 2118.

4

Place	Date	Hour	Summary of Events and Information	Remarks and references to Appendices
BEAURAINS	30/4/17	8 am	OC Company + 2/Lt LETTH made a reconnaissance of portion of front held by [illegible] Division Especially with regard to view from observation post at the end of a long sap in O 31. central	[illegible]
		9 am	Transport reached camp.	
		NOON	4 guns mounted for A A purposes round camp	

[illegible signature]
Major

A5834 Wt. W4973/M687 750,000 8/16 D. D. & L. Ltd. Forms/C.2118/13.

Vol 15

War Diary

for

May 1917.

53 M. G. Company

[illegible signature]

Ref Map 51. B. S.W. (1:20.000)

Instructions regarding War Diaries and Intelligence Summaries are contained in F. S. Regs., Part II. and the Staff Manual respectively. Title pages will be prepared in manuscript.

WAR DIARY
or
~~INTELLIGENCE SUMMARY.~~
(Erase heading not required.)

53rd M.G. Coy

Army Form C. 2118.

Place	Date	Hour	Summary of Events and Information	Remarks and references to Appendices
BEAURAINS	1st May		In bivouacs in M.10.b. Lt SHOTTER. 2/Lt CAESAR 2/Lt ALLAN reconnoitred Divisional front.	[initials]
NEUVILLE VITASSE	2nd May		Moved to area N.19 a. (NEUVILLE VITASSE) bivouaced in trench. (TWIG TR)	[initials]
"	3 "	4am	No 1 Section left camp to move to front line in readiness to garrison strong points in O.31 in the event of the ~~complete~~ success of attack of 54 & 55 Brigades. Reached front line 6.45 am. Owing to the attack not being successful, this section remained in CURTAIN TR all day. Shelling heavy no casualties one gun blown out of emplacement but undamaged.	
"	"	12.30 P.M.	6th Royal Berks moved forward to Support Positions round N.30b. 2 guns No 3 Section 2/Lt CAESAR ~~accompanied~~ were attached to them, their guns moving independently via and HENINEL (pack mules to HENINEL) Guns dug in near QUARRY N.30 b 9.1. 2 guns (No 3 Section) (2/Lt JONES) moved forward in conjunction with 8th SUFFOLKS to positions at N.30 c 8.5 ~~& central~~ & 95.65	
"		10 pm	No 4 Section (2/Lt ALLAN) moved forward in conjunction with 10 ESSEX to reserve positions on line N.27 b 65 – N.22 central 2 guns on extreme left 2 guns on extreme right of this line	
"		11 pm	Their Guns in position and in touch with 10 Essex	[initials]

[signature] Major

A5834 Wt. W4973/M687 750,000 8/16 D. D. & L. Ltd. Forms/C.2118/13.

Ref Map 51.B S.W. 1/20000

Instructions regarding War Diaries and Intelligence Summaries are contained in F. S. Regs., Part II. and the Staff Manual respectively. Title pages will be prepared in manuscript.

WAR DIARY
or
~~INTELLIGENCE SUMMARY.~~
(Erase heading not required.)

53rd M.G. Coy

Army Form C. 2118.

Place	Date	Hour	Summary of Events and Information	Remarks and references to Appendices
NEUVILLE-VITASSE	4th May	11.30 am	~~Arranged~~ O.C. Coy ~~met~~ G.O.C. 53 Bde at N.22d 5.5 (HQ 54 & 55 Bdes) and arranged to relieve 54 & 55 M.G. Coys in the line on evening 4 May.	
			No 1 Section, already in ~~Curtain~~ CURTAIN TR, closed to the left and took over from 55 M.G. Coy. This relief complete by 8 pm. H.Q. No 1 Section O.25.d 5.5	
			No 3 Section from area N.30 relieved 54 Company in CURTAIN TRENCH.	
			No 4 Section moved forward with 10th ESSEX and occupied positions in N.30.	
			No 2 Section occupied positions vacated by No 4 Section.	
		7pm	Company HQ moved to SUNKEN ROAD N.22d 5.5 (with Bde HQ)	[initials]
			Position of Company at 12 midnight 4/5th shewn on attached map.	MAP 'A'
N.22.d.	5 May	–	Guns in front line resited and position altered consequent on Bde taking up to sunken road in O.31.d	" "
			Heavy shelling of front line. Tripod of No 4 gun No 3 Section damaged. No 1 Section 2 casualties. No 2 Section gun team at N.22a 7.3 struck by a shell. 3 casualties.	
			During night two guns No 3 Section in sap struck by shrapnel and put out of action. Two guns sent over by No 1 Section to replace them	[initials]
	6 –	8am	No 2 Section relieved No 1 Section in left front line. No 1 Section reached Bde HQ. at 11am.	

[signature]

A5834 Wt. W4973/M687 750,000 8/16 D. D. & L. Ltd. Forms/C.2118/13.

ETERPIGNY SHEET 1/20,000

Instructions regarding War Diaries and Intelligence Summaries are contained in F. S. Regs., Part II. and the Staff Manual respectively. Title pages will be prepared in manuscript.

WAR DIARY or ~~INTELLIGENCE~~ SUMMARY.

(Erase heading not required.)

53 M. G. Coy

Army Form C. 2118.

Place	Date	Hour	Summary of Events and Information	Remarks and references to Appendices
N.22d	6 May Contd	12 noon	Company HQ moved to N.30c 3.4	
		8 pm	No 4 section relieved No 3 Section ~~in~~ in right front sector. No 3 section returned to support positions.	
N.30c 3.4	7 May	–	Machine Gun positions of area organised finally as shown in Map A. Work commenced at these positions. Shafts ~~put in~~ commenced by R.E. at PELICAN LANE the long sap in O.31 central* and gun at O 25.b 95.05	*: later LARK LANE
"	8 "	–	Positions as above. No change in situation. ~~No 1 Section~~ ~~[illegible]~~ ~~[illegible]~~ ~~[illegible]~~ ~~[illegible]~~ ~~[illegible]~~ ~~[illegible]~~ ~~[illegible]~~ Two men wounded at (one returned to duty)	
"	9 "	–	No change in positions. No 3 Section commenced digging positions for indirect fire at N.36.c.5.5.	
"	10 "	–	Situation unchanged in morning. At noon ordered to close to right taking over from ~~[illegible]~~ 63 M.G. Coy ~~[illegible]~~ 21 Division up to HINDENBURG line while 14 Division took over left sector up to CABLE TR in O.25 d. No 1 Section was moved from Reserve to relief of 63 M.G. Coy. 45 M.G. Coy relieved No 2 Section on left this section being withdrawn to reserve.	
		10.15 p	Double relief complete 10.15 pm	
"	11	–	Company HQ moved to HINDENBURG SUPPORT LINE at T.5.c.7.8 move complete by 6.20 pm.	

A5834 Wt. W4973/M687 750,000 8/16 D. D. & L. Ltd. Forms/C.2118/13.

[signature]

Ref 51 B . SW. 1/20.000

Instructions regarding War Diaries and Intelligence Summaries are contained in F. S. Regs., Part II. and the Staff Manual respectively. Title pages will be prepared in manuscript.

WAR DIARY
or
~~INTELLIGENCE SUMMARY.~~
(*Erase heading not required.*)

53 M. G. Coy

Army Form C. 2118.

Place	Date	Hour	Summary of Events and Information	Remarks and references to Appendices
T.5.6.7.8	11 oct	9.30	No 3 Section fired with two guns on area O.3.2.6.E.	Map B
		–	Positions of guns now as in MAP B	[initials]
–"–	12 –		No 2 Section moved up from reserve and took over from No 1 Section on right. No 1 Section moved to left & took over from No 4 Section who came into reserve in HINDENBURG line.	[initials]
–"–	13 –		Situation as above unchanged Working on emplacements	[initials]
–"–	14 –	–	Unchanged. No 3 Section fired at night	[initials]
–"–	15 –	–	Situation as above unchanged. Transport lines moved from Sugar Factory NEUVILLE VITASSE to T.2.a.3.3 (HENIN-SUR COJEUL).	
		6 pm	O.C. Coy reported to G.O.C. Bde and accompanied him to 33 Divisional conference with a view to assisting a proposed attack of that division with MG fire	[initials]
–"–	16 –	9.30 –	Conference of Section Commanders. Work all day preparing emplacements for covering fire. 4 in CURTAIN TR 4 in BROWN TR 4 in N.36 c 4 5	MAP B [initials]
–"–	17	–	Situation unchanged Work continued	[initials]
–"–	18	–	Reinforcement of 11 men arrived in trenches Work continued	[initials]

[signature] Major

A5834 Wt. W4973/M687 750,000 8/16 D. D. & L. Ltd. Forms/C.2118/13.

Map 51. B S.W. 1/20000

Army Form C. 2118.

Instructions regarding War Diaries and Intelligence Summaries are contained in F. S. Regs., Part II. and the Staff Manual respectively. Title pages will be prepared in manuscript.

WAR DIARY
or
~~INTELLIGENCE~~ SUMMARY.
(*Erase heading not required.*)

53 M.G. Coy

Place	Date	Hour	Summary of Events and Information	Remarks and references to Appendices
T.5.6.7.8	19 May	–	Work continued ammunition brought up & all arrangements made for barrage fire. No 4 section (reserve) took over left gun in Concrete TRENCH and then withdrew as 98 M.G. Coy mounted 7 guns in the trench.	[initials]
–"–	20 May	5.45 a	Guns fired on lines as indicated in Map B. 1 belt per gun per [illegible] minute	Map B
		6. a	Ceased fire	
		(3 am	Two men killed in Brown Tr. No 2 Section) One man wounded BROWN TR.	
		6 am	No 1 Section shelled 2 men wounded 1 gun tripod etc completely blown up. Attack of 33 Division not completely successful. Advice of enemy	
		11.15 a	massing. Guns therefore reopened	
		12.15	ceased fire again.	
			Belts refilled. 33 Division attacked again in the evening, our guns fired on same barrage lines as the morning	
		7.30 pm	Opened fire	
		8.15 pm	Ceased fire. No 1 Section had one gun put out of action with shrapnel.	[initials]
–"–	21st	12.10 a	33 Division asked for night firing along barrage lines. This done by 3 guns No 3 Section.	
		3 a.	No 1 Section opened fire for short time.	
			Ammunition expended during 33 Division operations No 1 Section 23.000 rounds. No 2 Section 20 000 No 3 Section 25.250 rounds = 68.250.	[signature]

A5834 Wt. W4973/M687 750,000 8/16 D. D. & L. Ltd. Forms/C.2118/13.

Army Form C. 2118.

Instructions regarding War Diaries and Intelligence Summaries are contained in F. S. Regs., Part II. and the Staff Manual respectively. Title pages will be prepared in manuscript.

WAR DIARY
or
INTELLIGENCE SUMMARY.
(Erase heading not required.)

Place	Date	Hour	Summary of Events and Information	Remarks and references to Appendices
T.5.b.7.8	21st May	3.30 pm	Relief of company by 55 MG Company commenced	
		7.15	Relief complete no casualties & comfortable relief	[illegible]
			Sections marched back independently to S.17 central camp	
S.17.	22nd	–	Rested in camp. Guns cleaned. Two anti-aircraft guns mounted	[illegible]
			Company bathed in afternoon	[illegible]
"	23		Rested	
"	24	–	~~Rested strong points in B line reconnoitred by OC Cy & 3 Section officers~~	[illegible]
		5.15	Brigade Conference	
"	25	–	Rested. B line reconnoitred by OC Cy & ~~[illegible]~~ 4 section officers	[illegible]
"	26	–	Training. Remaining officers reconnoitre routes to Strong Points in B line	[illegible]
"	27	–	Training. Sunday Divine Service	[illegible]
"	28	8-12 2-3	Training	
			Baths in Evening	[illegible]
"	29.	–	Training ~~stopped~~ altered owing to bad weather. One section [illegible] with 8 Norfolks	[illegible]

A5834 Wt. W4973/M687 750,000 8/16 D. D. & L. Ltd. Forms/C.2118/13.

Map 51.B S.W.

Instructions regarding War Diaries and Intelligence Summaries are contained in F. S. Regs., Part II. and the Staff Manual respectively. Title pages will be prepared in manuscript.

WAR DIARY
or
~~INTELLIGENCE~~ SUMMARY.
(Erase heading not required.)

53 M. G. Coy

Army Form C. 2118.

Place	Date	Hour	Summary of Events and Information	Remarks and references to Appendices
S17.c	30	-	Training.	
		3.30 p	Inspection by G.O.C. VII Corps.	
"	31	-	Nos 1 & 3 Sections cooperated with training 7/10 ESSEX	

[signature]

A5834 Wt. W4973/M687 750,000 8/16 D. D. & L. Ltd. Forms/C.2118/13.

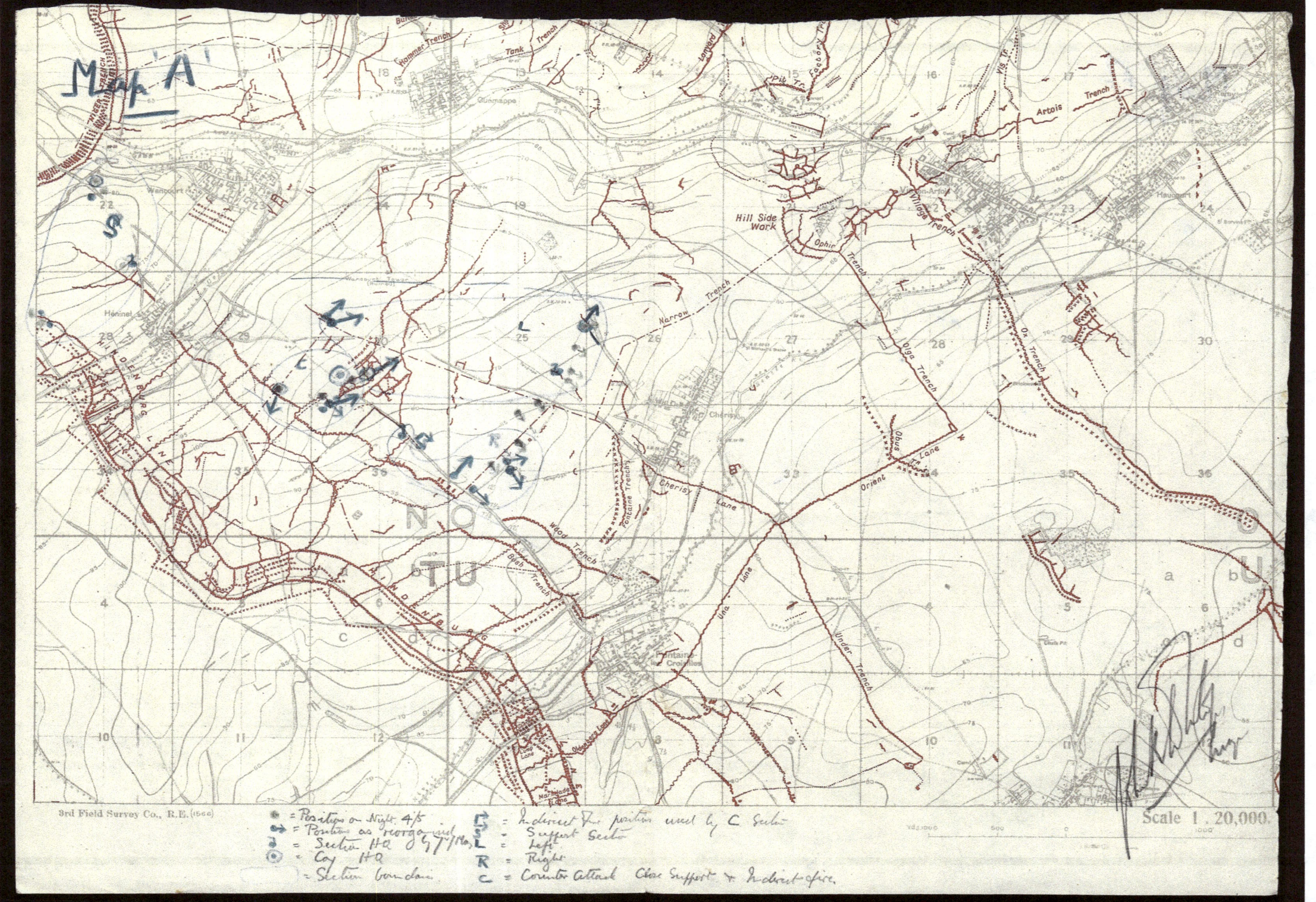
Map 'A'
Hommer Trench
Tank Trench
Guémappe
Artois Trench
Hill Side Work
Ophir Trench
Village Trench
Narrow Trench
Olga Trench
Ox Trench
Obus Lane
Orient Lane
Cherisy
Cherisy Lane
Fontaine Trench
Wood Trench
Bush Trench
Una Lane
Under Trench
Héninel
Wancourt
Haucourt
Fontaine Croisilles
HINDENBURG LINE
3rd Field Survey Co., R.E. (566)
Scale 1 . 20,000.
= Position on Night 4/5
= Position as reorganised by 7th/Mar
= Section HQ
= Coy HQ
= Section boundaries
= Indirect fire position used by C Section
S = Support Section
L = Left
R = Right
C = Counter attack Close Support + Indirect fire.

Map 'A'

Appendix to
WAR DIARY
May 1917.

53 M.G. Coy

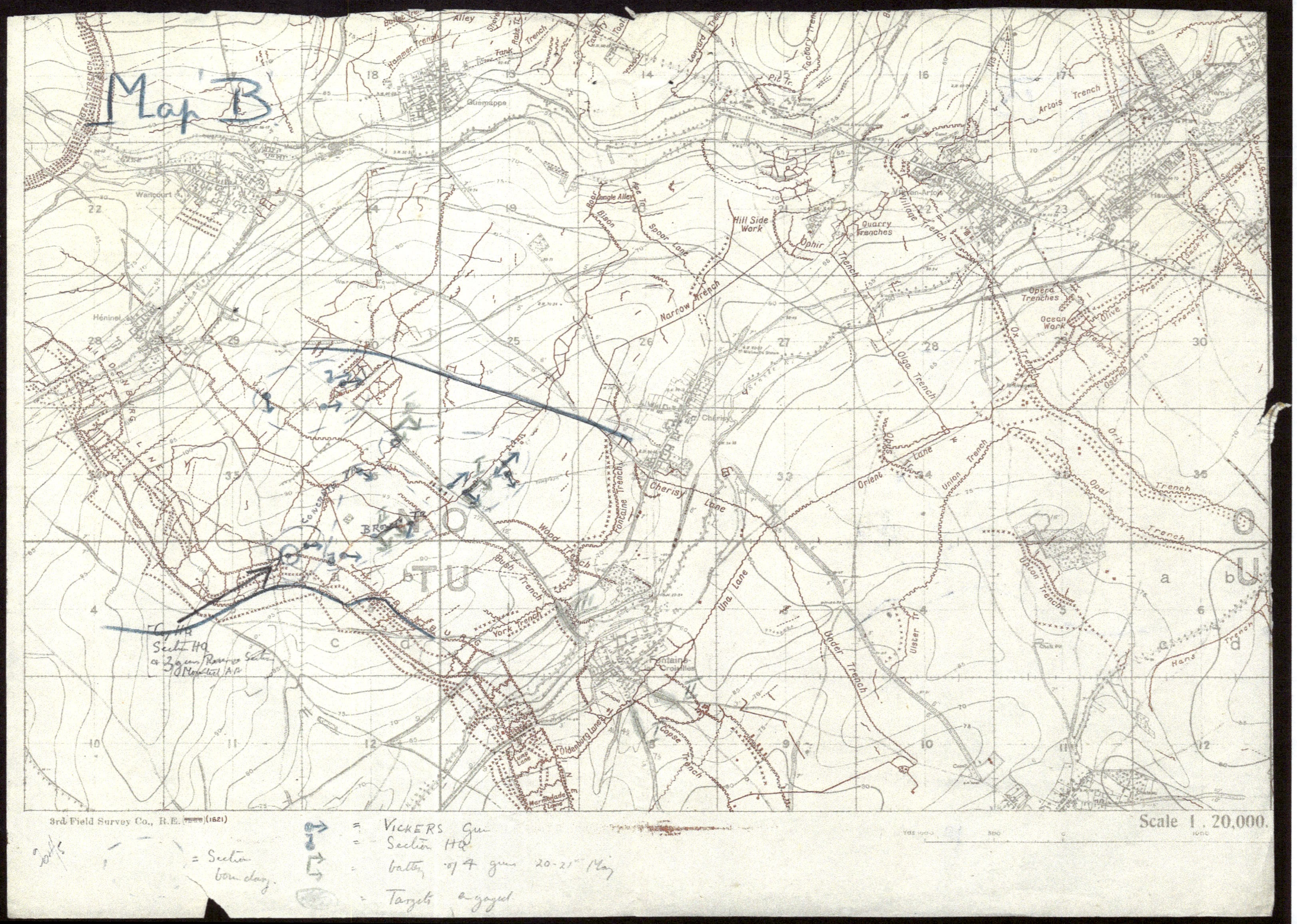

Map B
Hammer Trench
Alley
Tank
Trench
Guemappe
Cavalry
Lanyard Trench
Pic Tr.
Factory Trench
Artois Trench
Wancourt
Boar
Jungle Alley
Ape Tr.
Bison
Spoor Lane
Hill Side Work
Ophir Trench
Quarry Trenches
Village Trench
Opera Trenches
Ocean Work
Olive
Héninel
Narrow Trench
Olga Trench
Ox Trench
Orix
Chérisy
Fontaine Trench
Cherisy Lane
Obus
Lane
Orient
Union Trench
Opal
Trench
Wood Trench
Bush Trench
York Trench
Una Lane
Under Trench
Ulster Tr.
Upton Trench
Hans
Trench
Fontaine-lès-Croisilles
Oldenburg Lane
Copse Trench
Section HQ
& 3 gun Ranging Section
3rd Field Survey Co., R.E. (1621)
Scale 1 . 20,000.
= VICKERS Gun
= Section HQ
= battery of 4 guns 20–21st May
= Targets engaged
= Section boundary

Map B

Appendix
to War Diary
May 1917.

53 M.G. Coy.

Ref. Map 51B. S.W 1/20.000

June 1917.

Army Form C. 2118.

WAR DIARY
or
~~INTELLIGENCE SUMMARY.~~ 53 M.G Coy

(Erase heading not required.)

Vol 16

Instructions regarding War Diaries and Intelligence Summaries are contained in F. S. Regs., Part II. and the Staff Manual respectively. Title pages will be prepared in manuscript.

Place	Date	Hour	Summary of Events and Information	Remarks and references to Appendices
S17 central	1st Jun	–	Training. Brigade Operations W of MERCATEL	[initials]
	2"	10am	Demonstration of Bombing Attack by Bde Bombing School	
		4.30pm	Company Moved ~~[illegible]~~ (sections independently at 15 mins interval to Support area taking over from 54 M.G. Coy	[initials]
M.36 b.	3"	–	Parade for adjustment of stores. Two A.A. guns mounted	[initials]
– " –	4	9am	Training. Reconnaissance of 'B' line by 1+2 Sections.	[initials]
– " –	5	9.30am	Company at baths No 3+4 Sections reconnoitred 'B' line	[initials]
– " –	6	9am	Nos 3+4 Sections on Range	
		6pm	The Coy reconnoitred 42 Bde Sector (portion from O.31.b.4.9. to O.26.a.58) with Bde & Major	[initials]
– " –	7	9am	Parade	
		1pm	Nos 1+2 Sections on Range ~~[illegible]~~	[initials]
– " –	8		Lt Coates & 2/Lt Jones reconnoitred line with O.C. Coy	
		7pm	Digging & carrying parties up working on Nos 2+5 positions.	Map A [initials]
– " –	9	2-6pm	Baths.	
		–	Completion of work on 2+5 positions, which were being prepared for Divisional Enfilade Fire Scheme.	[initials]

A5834 Wt. W4973/M687 750,000 8/16 D. D. & L. Ltd. Forms/C.2118/13.

Map 'A'
Tank Trench
Hammer Trench
Guémappe
Lanyard
Pelican Trench
Artois Trench
Vis. Tr.
Hill Side Work
Ophir Trench
Village Trench
Wancourt
Héninel
Narrow Trench
Olga Trench
Ox Trench
Obus
Orient Lane
Cherisy
Cherisy Lane
Fontaine Trench
Wood Trench
Bush Trench
Una Lane
Under Trench
Fontaine-les-Croisilles
HINDENBURG LINE
Scale 1 : 20,000.
3rd Field Survey Co., R.E.
• = Positions on Night 4/5
= Positions as reorganised by 7th Mx
= Section HQ
= Coy HQ
= Section boundary
= Indirect fire positions used by C Section
S = Support Section
L = Left
R = Right
C = Counter attack Close Support + Indirect fire.

Map 'A'

Appendix to
WAR DIARY
May 1917.

53 M.G. Coy

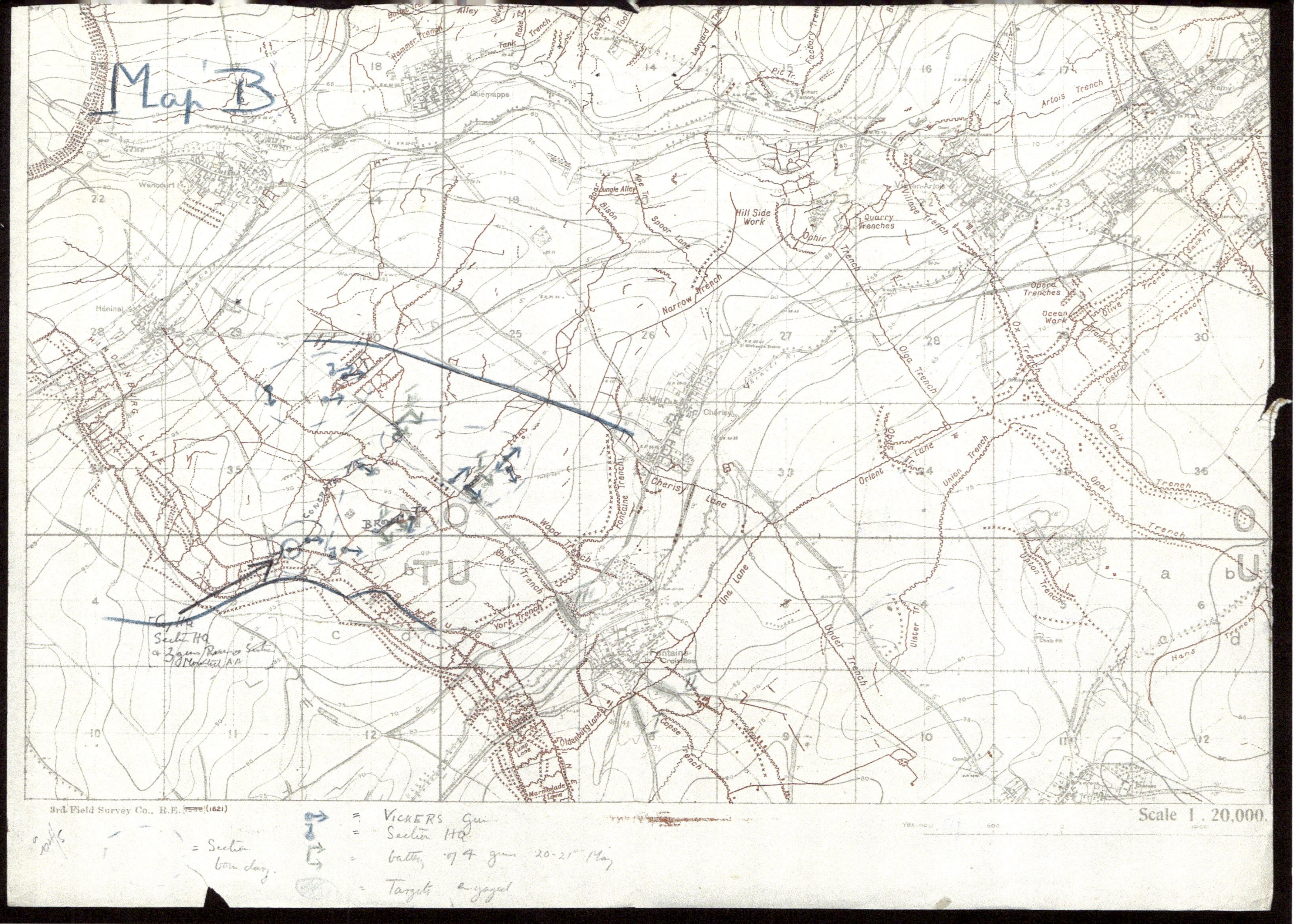

Map 'B'
Scale 1. 20,000.
3rd Field Survey Co., R.E. (1621)
= VICKERS Gun
= Section HQ
= battery of 4 guns 20-21st May
= Section boundary
= Targets engaged
Section HQ
Artois Trench
Village Trench
Quarry Trenches
Hill Side Work
Ophir Trench
Spoar Lane
Narrow Trench
Jungle Alley
Bison
Ape Tr.
Opera Trenches
Ocean Work
Ox Trench
Olga Trench
Orix Trench
Opal Trench
Orient Lane
Union Trench
Upton Trench
Ulster Tr.
Under Trench
Une Lane
Cherisy Lane
Fontaine Trench
Wood Trench
Bush Trench
York Trench
Copse Trench
Oldenburg Lane
Hans Trench
Cherisy
Fontaine-Croisilles
Guémappe
Wancourt
Héninel
Hammer Trench
Tank Trench
Lanyard Trench
Pic Tr.
Factory Trench

Map B

Appendix
to War Diary
May 1917.

53 Mg. Coy.

Ref: Map LENS 11 1/100 000

Instructions regarding War Diaries and Intelligence Summaries are contained in F. S. Regs., Part II. and the Staff Manual respectively. Title pages will be prepared in manuscript.

WAR DIARY
or
INTELLIGENCE SUMMARY.
(Erase heading not required.)

Army Form C. 2118.

Place	Date	Hour	Summary of Events and Information	Remarks and references to Appendices
SOUASTRE	19	-	NO PARADES - COY RESTING.	[illegible]
"	20	8.30am to 12.30am	Coy Training	[illegible]
"	21	"	" "	[illegible]
"	22	"	" "	[illegible]
"	23	"	"	[illegible]
"	24		Sunday. Lt [illegible] accompanied Bde Commander on visit to "Somme Battlefields"	[illegible]
"	25		Coy Training.	[illegible]
"			Coy Route March.	
"	26			[illegible]
"	27		Coy. Training	[illegible]
"	28		Do Do	[illegible]
"	29		Do	[illegible]
"	30			

A5834 Wt. W4973/M687 750,000 8/16 D. D. & L. Ltd. Forms/C.2118/13.

Instructions regarding War Diaries and Intelligence Summaries are contained in F. S. Regs., Part II. and the Staff Manual respectively. Title pages will be prepared in manuscript.

WAR DIARY or ~~INTELLIGENCE SUMMARY.~~

(Erase heading not required.)

The 53rd M. G. Company

Army Form C. 2118.

Vol 17

Place	Date	Hour	Summary of Events and Information	Remarks and references to Appendices
SOUASTRE.	1/7/17		Sunday — Church Parades.	[illegible]
"	2/7/17		Training — [illegible]	[illegible]
"	3/7/17		Coy moved to new area. Entrained at MONDICOURT 8.50 am. Arrived CASSEL and marched to billets in K.14.d (ref. map HAZEBRUCK) STEENVORDE AREA.	[illegible]
STEENVORDE AREA	4/7/17		Resting in billets.	[illegible]
"	5/7/17		Coy Training.	[illegible]
"	6/7/17		Inspection by Corps Commander.	[illegible]
"	7/7/17		Coy Training.	[illegible]
"	8/7/17		Sunday. — Church Service.	[illegible]
"	9/7/17		Coy Training	[illegible]
"	10/7/17		-Do- — One officer and 5 O.R. proceeded to ANTI-AIRCRAFT Course	[illegible]
"	11/7/17		-Do- Afternoon. — Coy Sports.	[illegible]
"	12/7/17		-Do-	[illegible]
"	13/7/17		-Do-	[illegible]
"	14/7/17		-Do- Billets moved to K.21.b.7.3 (Baton Farm)	[illegible]
"	15/7/17		Sunday.	[illegible]
"	16/7/17		No. 1 Section relieve ANTI-AIRCRAFT guard at OUDER-DOM DUMP. Remainder of Coy [illegible] training	[illegible]

A5834 Wt. W4973/M687 750,000 8/16 D. D. & L. Ltd. Forms/C.2118/13.

Instructions regarding War Diaries and Intelligence Summaries are contained in F. S. Regs., Part II. and the Staff Manual respectively. Title pages will be prepared in manuscript.

WAR DIARY
or
~~INTELLIGENCE~~ SUMMARY.

(*Erase heading not required.*)

Army Form C. 2118.

Place	Date	Hour	Summary of Events and Information	Remarks and references to Appendices
STEENVOORDE AREA	17/7/17		Coy training	
	18/7/17		Do.	
	19/7/17		Do.	
	20/7/17		No2 section joined No1 section at OUDERDOM & proceeded to relieve eight guns of 85 Coy in the line	
	21/7/17		Coy training	
	22/7/17		Sunday	
	23/7/17		Coy training	
	24/7/17		Two sections holding the line were relieved & came back to OTTAWA CAMP (85 Coys billets)	
	25/7/17		Coy training	
	26/7/17		Two sections rejoined the Company from OTTAWA CAMP.	
	27/7/17		Coy training	
	28/7/17		Coy moved up to RENINGHELST STAGING AREA	
	29/7/17		Coy moved forward to NEW DICKEBUSCH CAMP. Two sections	

A5834 Wt. W4973/M687 750,000 8/16 D. D. & L. Ltd. Forms/C.2118/13.

Army Form C. 2118.

Instructions regarding War Diaries and Intelligence Summaries are contained in F. S. Regs., Part II. and the Staff Manual respectively. Title pages will be prepared in manuscript.

WAR DIARY
or
~~INTELLIGENCE SUMMARY.~~

(*Erase heading not required.*)

Place	Date	Hour	Summary of Events and Information	Remarks and references to Appendices
	2[illegible]/7/17		Lt Gray [illegible] BARRAGE during Operations moved into positions in MAPLE TRENCH to make final preparations.	
	2[illegible]/7/17		HQ moved up to RIDGE STREET forward BDE H.Q. for Operation No 4 Section reported to 8th NORFOLK REGT to assist in Consolidation of ground gained.	
			Half No 3 Section attached 6th R. BERKS to assist assault	
			Half – " – " – 8th SUFFOLKS Do.	
	[illegible]/7/17		ZERO HOUR 3.50 am.	
			Operations [illegible]	

A5834 Wt. W4973/M687 750,000 8/16 D. D. & L. Ltd. Forms/C.2118/13.

53 LTMY5.

YPRES OPERATIONS

------July 3rd. to 31st. 1917.---

July 3rd. The Battalion left the ARRAS Area by train, arrived at CASSEL at 7.30am. on the 4th. and marched to billets and bivouacs in farms about the STEENVOORDE Area.

July 4th. All Officers were addressed by the 2nd. Corps Commander - (Lieut. General JACOBS. K.C.B.) on the subject of the forthcoming operations.

July 6th. to 24th. Training of all sorts was carried out on areas and such places as were available and suitable.
Brigade, Battalion and Company Conferences were continually being held. Parties of Officers, N.C.O's and men were daily visiting the forward area, and a model of the ground near BUSSE - BOOM and were conveyed to and from by Motor Lorries.

July 25th. The Battalion was due to leave the STEENVOORDE Area at 10.45pm. this was cancelled at about 5pm.
Battalion Operation Orders for the forthcoming Operations were issued early in the morning.

July 26th. At 11.45am. the Brigadier (Brigadier-General Higginson D.S.O.) addressed the Battalion on the subject of the forthcoming operations, expressing his complete confidence in them and wishing them every possible good fortune.

July 28th. The Battalion left Billets at 10pm. and marched to a Camp at G.32.c. near RENINGHELST (Belguim, Sheet 28.1/20,000.N.W.). where it arrived at 1.30am. on the 29th.
Heavy thunderstorm at 7am. rain lasted till 12 noon.

July 29th. At 3pm. the final conference was held at Brigade Headquarters
The Battalion left this Camp at 7.30pm. and marched by Companies to NEW DICKEBUSCH CAMP where it arrived at 10.30pm.

July 30th. A nice fine morning early, but this soon turned into a steady drizzle which lasted till 11am. when the rain ceased. The Battalion left this Camp by platoons for the forward Assembly Area in the following order, starting at 9.30pm. "A" Coy. "B" Coy. H.Q. Coy. "D" Coy. T.M. Battery (1 gun team) "C" Coy. half section M.G. Coy.
The Blue track which was picketed under 2nd. Lt. N. Bolingbroke by N.C.O's and men from the "Details" was followed throughout. The night was comparatively quiet as regards enemy shelling. The Battalion only suffered when "C" Coy. reached ZILLIBEKE VILLAGE.

July 31st. The whole Battalion was located in the forward assemble Area. (Details, Operation Order No.30) by 2am. At this hour and up till "Zero Hour" the enemy shell fire appreciably increased. "ZERO HOUR" was 3.50am.
At this hour the light was distinctly bad, visibility being only possible for a very short distance. From this Point onwards I will deal with Battalion Headquarters, each Company, 1 gun T.M. Battery and the half section M.G. Company in detail, finishing with a few general remarks and a list of the casualties.

B A T T A L I O N   H E A D Q U A R T E R S

At "Zero Hour" Battalion Headquarters was established in WELLINGTON CRESCENT. At 7.20am.Headquarters started to move forward with a view to establishing themselves at J.14.a.4.3. or that vicinity. A heavy enemy barrage was encountered in SANCTUARY WOOD and on the eastern edge Machine Gun and Rifle fire was met.

The first halt was made on the line of JACKDAW RESERVE where it was seen that the enemy were holding YPRES - MENIN ROAD, western edge of GLENCORSE WOOD and Strong Point J.14.a.3.3. this was at about 8.10am.

Headquarters were eventually moved up to about J.13.b.5.0. where they were established by 9.15am.

A visual signal station was established at about J.13.d.8.7. At about 2.30pm.Headquarters were moved to the Tunnell under the YPRES - MENIN ROAD,at about J.13.b.2.3.

The Battalion Scouts under Lieut.R.C.BOLINGBROKE had moved forward at 6am.to assist in marking out the route forward. As they encountered practically none of the 90th.Brigade Lieut.BOLINGBROKE decided to gain what information he could. He reached the BLUE LINE about J.13.b.6.3. where he was wounded in the head and shoulder,he remained at duty until he could do nothing further.

The work performed by Lieut.BOLINGBROKE, as on all occasions been most conspicuous,and on this occasion it was as usual marked by great gallantry,determination and disregard of everything personal in order to gain information and assist the operations.

Battalion Headquarters eventually left J.13.b.2.3. at about 4am.on Morning August 1st.arrived at the vicinity of RITZ STREET at about 5.30am. and at the Camp at DICKEBUSCHE at about (am.

I particularly wish to place on record the gallant and admirable work performed by the following throughout these operations.

Capt. & Adjt. G.L.M.Fache. M.C.
Lieut. R.C. Bolingbroke.
3/9691. R.S.M. W. Goody.
14791.Pte. P.Leader.
14684.Pte. C.C.Arbin.
14520.Pte. W.J.Riches.

"A" COMPANY

The Company left the forward assembly area (NORMAN TRENCH) at 7am. in the following order,

Company Headqyarters .
Nos.2 and 4 Platoons 1st.Line.
No.3.Platoon 2nd.Line.
No.4.Platoon 3rd.Line.

A certain amount of loss of direction occurred at the commencement but this was eventually rectified and by the time the MENIN ROAD was reached the left of the Company was on more or less its allotted front. The frontage covered by the Coy.was not however as large as was intended but this under the corcumstances was unavoidable. The enemy's barrage was encountered in SANCTUARY WOOD & in addition M.G.Fire from GLENCORSE WOOD & the MENIN ROAD and these inflicted the first casualties on the Company. Close to the MENIN ROAD an Officer of the Manchester Regt.was metwho said that GLENCORSE WOOD was in our hands,he was one of the very few of the 90th.Brigade(30th. Division)seen throughout the day on the Battalion Frontage,his information was however soon contradicted by Lieut.BOLINGBROKE.The enemy were obviously holding much of the ground to the West of GLENCORSE WOOD. Nos.2 and 4 Platoons under 2nd.Lieut.MASTIN were now ordered to advance by sections and make good the ridge S.E. of SURBITON VILLAS,these platoons were followed by Nos.1 & 3 under 2nd.Lieut.WHEELER. Good progress was made for about 300 yards when the line was held up by M.G.Fire from the right. No.18182.Pte.READ.F. and a few other men put this gun out of action & killed the team on their own initiative & this allowed the advance to again continue to the ridge in question. Progress was however slow throughout owing to heavy M.G. & Rifle Fire which necessitated the advance being carried out from shell hole to shell hole.
From this position no further progress was possible as the enemy's M.G.Fire & Rifle Fire was too heavy & accurate. An attempt was made by 2nd.Lieut.WHEELER under covering fire from the left directed by Lieut.BOLINGBROKE to advance,but casualties were too heavy,2nd.Lieut. WHEELER among others being killed in the attempt. 2 sections of No.4. Platoon further to the right with "C" Coy.were able to push forward but these were later forced to withdraw owing to our own heavies firing short. Four Tanks now made their appearance and made most gallant attempts to get forward,they were all in turn knocked out by heavy enemy shell fire directed against them.
It was now decided to dig in and consolidate as well as possible the ground gained,but this work was much hindered by M.G. & shell fire. The latter becoming both accurate & severe after enemy areoplanes flying low had reconnoitred our positions. All these planes were heavily fired on by rifles,L.G. & M.G'S but were not apparently brought down. At about 8.30pm.orders as to the relief by the 19th. K.L.R. were received & the Coy.eventually moved back at midnight. During the whole of these operations the behaviour of all ranks was throughout beyond praise. Officers & N.C.O's grasped the situation & acted with promptness,judgement & determination.
The features of the ground were made good use of & every opportunity of inflicting to the enemy & assisting the advance by rifle fire was seized. I particularly wish to place on record the gallant & valuable work per formed throughout by the following;-

Capt.H.A.Angier.M.C. 2nd.Lt.J.D.Wheeler(Killed) 2nd.Lt.S.L.A.Mastin.
3/9732.C.S.M.D.Wells. 3/9686.Sgt.T.Eaves. 14174.Sgt.C.Smith.
12882.Cpl.H.J.Westley. 18182.Pte.F.Read. 13986.Pte.S.G.Smith.
14050.Pte.J.Lucas. 14478. Pte.O.Rainsford(Killed).

"B" COMPANY.

The Company started its advance in artillery formation from the forward assembly area at 7.45am.

Heavy enemy shell fire was encountered in SANCTUARY WOOD and at the Eastern edge some machine gun fire, the line of JACKDAW RESERVE was reached with very little loss.

From here it was found quite necessary to deploy & move by sections, the section Commanders in every case took command and lead their sections with ability and confidence.

On reaching the vicinity of SURBITON VILLAS fighting became particularly heavy, casualties occuring frequently from the enemy M.G. and rifle fire.

All sections and particularly the Lewis Guns from this point did very good work against the enemy, the covering fire was accurate, well directed and controlled. The advance onwards was purely a matter of rushes, chiefly from shell hole to shell hole, touch was maintained right and left throughout & eventually the line was forced to halt about 200 yards East of SURBITON VILLAS. It was during this advance that Lieut. R.S. CHIBNALL was killed. This line was held till about 2pm, when, through heavy enemy shelling & our own heavies firing short it was forced to withdraw with the left in touch with the 6th. Royal Berkshire Regt. at about J.13.b.8.4. I cannot speak too highly of the keenness, determination, pluck, and gallantry displayed by all ranks of the Company during a very severe and hard fought action.

The relief of the Coy. was completed by about 1am. August 1st.

I particularly wish to place on record the valuable work performed by the following.

Capt. E.J. Greene. M.C.
Lieut. R.S. Chibnall. (Killed).
2nd. Lieut. L.P. Pells.
2nd. Lieut. G.G. Hannan.
3/8662. Sgt. A.E. Norris.
3/10115. Sgt. G.W. Pooley.
15401. Sgt. C. Brookes.
16103. Cpl. W.G. Batchelor.
18014. L/C. A.W. Wright.
25008. L/C. H. Impey.
40442. L/C. J. Osborne.
14688. L/C., G.H. Mayes.
14103. L/C. W. Davey.
14971. Pte. H. Doy.

"C" COMPANY.

The Coy. unfortunately lost 5 men killed & 3 wounded in addition to 1 Lewis Gun in ZILLIBEKE on the way up to the forward assembly area on night of 30th. At 7.10am. the Coy. formed up in Artillery formation and left the assembly trenches about 150 yards behind the support Coy. at 7.20am. Through SANCTUARY WOOD the enemy barrage was very heavy & the M.G. fire on the Eastern Edge was distinctly heavy. Platoon Commanders shewed good judgement during this advance in the observation of the enemy shell fire. On arrival at the MENIN ROAD the entire frantage of the Battalion was not occupied & it was found necessary to prolong the line to the right in order to, both occupy our frontage & gain touch with the 17th. K.L.R. on our right. No one of the 90th. Brigade (30th. Division) was met during the advance of the Company up to and beyond the MENIN ROAD, the only information obtainable was from our own observation & 2nd. Lt. Hannan (Patrol Guide), who was met on the MENIN ROAD. Progress beyond the MENIN ROAD was held up by M.G. fire & rifle fire from the strong point J.14.a.3.3. until one Stokes Gun was brought into action. Under cover from this & fire from the M.G. attached to the Battalion & rifle fire the Coy. was able to push forward. The advance to JAP AVENUE was successfully accomplished & here a temporary halt was necessary. Rifle and L.G. fire together with rifle grenades were now directed against the enemy strong point & on a trench in the Sunken Road (J.14.a). & when the situation appeared favourable a further advance to within 100 yards of the strong point was carried out. From here it was not possible to advance further & consolidation of shell holes was commenced, this was very considerably hampered by M.G. & Rifle Fire from the strong point J.14.a.3.3. GLENCORSE WOOD and INVERNESS COPSE. The Coy. was not now in touch with the 17th. K.L.R. on the right although our right flank was even over our boundary line. The position did not appear at all satisfactory & Lieut. Srgles decided to make an attempt to rush the strong point & thus strengthen the whole position. The attempt was partially successful, a footing was gained, 1 M.G. put out of action & 20 prisoners taken & a considerable number of the enemy killed. The Company on the left were not able to advance however & owing to this in addition to heavy enemy shell, M.G. & T.M. fire the line withdrew to its original position. Our own heavies were now falling short & coupled with the accurate & heavy enemy shelling directed by low flying aeroplanes made our position very uncomfortable & in fact absolutely untenable, & the line had to be still further withdrawn to JAP AVENUE where touch was now gained with the 17th. K.L.R. on the right. The Coy. was eventually relieved by the 19th. K.L.R. early on morning of August 1st. The fine spirit, unerring devotion to duty & determination to push on & give every assistance to other units in the face of very heavy fire, displayed by all ranks of this Coy. deserves the highest praise. The Coy. lost 1 Officer Killed (2nd. Lt. Savage), 1 Officer wounded (2nd. Lt. Rae) who however remained at duty throughout, & 5 Sgts. & I cannot speak too highly of 2nd. Lt. Argles, Commanding the Coy. & the junior N.C.O's who so ably filled the breach caused by senior casualties. It is exceedingly hard to single out individuals from a Coy. which did such magnificient work but the valuable services performed by the following are unquestionable.

2nd. Lt. C.A.C. Argles. 2nd. Lt. L.C. Rae. 2nd. Lt. A.C. Savage. (Killed).
14136. Sgt. A. Woollner. 14653. Sgt. H.J. Remblance.
13883. Sgt. E.S. Houghton. 14605. Cpl. J. Crompton.
18558. Cpl. F. Bowers. 22410. Pte. A. Champion.
16013. Pte. A. Elmer.

"D" COMPANY.

This Coy.was in support for the attack. It left the assembly trenches in artillery formation at 7.15am. In passing through SANCTUARY WOOD heavy enemy shell fire was encountered & the Coy.suffered numerous casualties. The line of the MENIN ROAD was reached about 8.45am.& up to this time practically no one of the 90th.Brigade(30th.Division) had been seen & the only information obtainable was from our own observation & our own guides who had preceded the Battalion. The Coy. was used to prolong to the right of "A" Coy.& kept touch with "C" Coy.on the right.The advance from the MENIN ROAD had to be carried out by rushes from shell hole to shell hole each advance assisted by covering rifle & L.G.Fire.The enemy's M.G. & rifle fire from the strong point at J.14.a.3.3.the trench running N.E.& JARGON TRENCH was both heavy & accurate & inflicted severe casualties & made the advance very slow.A line about 150 yards beyond the MENIN ROAD was reached & here Capt.Crandon was wounded,also 2nd.Lt.Brown,the latter however remained at duty with the Coy.throughout the operations & was executed after arrival in Camp on August 1st.The advance was continued slowly until it was found impossible in spite of many gallant attempts to continue owing to the very heavy M.G. & Rifle fire from the Strong Point & GLENCORSE WOOD. Touch was gained right & left & the work of consolidation was commenced on about the line J.13.b.9.2. - J.14.a.1.0. This work was by no means easy & the difficulties multiplied by the heavy M.G.fire & later by heavy & accurate shell fire directed by low flying hostile aeroplanes. Later on our heavies commenced to shell presumably the strong point ,out their range was considerably short. The Coy.was eventually relieved by the 19th.K.L.R.& left ~~xxx~~ at 2am.on morning of August 1st. The work performed by all ranks of the Coy.under most diffivult conditions was carried out with the utmost gallantry & determination.All ranks displayed the greatest keenness to get forward & if possible get to a position from which the Battalions allotted task could be carried out.

In placing on record the speIndid work of the following I only mention a very small proportion of the Coy.all of whom did most valuable work.

Capt.G.L.Crandon.M.C. who,although wounded remained at duty until he could do nothing further.

2nd.Lt.W.Brown.
2nd.Lt.F.C.J.Latham.
3/10273.Sgt.C.F.Tuttle.
6109.Sgt.P.Farrold.
15020.Sgt.C.K.Spindler.
3/10100.Cpl.T.Making.
14821.Cpl.E.J.Hazelwood.
14961.L/C.A.King.
3/9873.Pte.C.A.Wentworth.
15372.Pte.J.Sawyer.
13917.Pte.G.A.Long.
41076.Pte.C.W.Cox.
41088.Pte.A.Doodenham.
18303.Pte.H.T.Pollard.

Half Section 53rd.MACHINE GUN COMPANY.

This section under Lieut.J.C.Biggs.M.C.advanced from the assembly area with "C" Companyat 9125am.it was ~~xxxxxx~~ brought into action from about J.13.d.7.9. against the enemy strong point at J.14.a.3.3 It subsequently moved forward and was established about J.14.c.1.8. I particularly wish to draw attention to the excellent work done byoLieut.Biggs. He not only handled the half section throughout with the greatest ability,energy and determination under heavy shell,Machine Gun and rifle fire byt himself worked an enemy mortar against the strong point with good effect.

---

1 Gun 53rd. TRENCH MORTAR BATTERY.

This gun under 2nd.Lt.H.S.walters and 14110.Cpl.E.Nunn advancdd with the Headquarters of "D" Company.
4 carriers were lost on the advance to the MENIN ROAD and they arrived with only about 15 shells.
The gun was ably handled and brought into action at about 9.25am. from about J.13.d.6.6. against the strong point at J.14.a.3 3
It dealt with this very effectively was the range was accurately obtained and must have inflicted numerous casualties,as the enemy were seen to be obviously shaken and disorganized while the shells were available. With an adequate supply of shells for this gun the strong point could have been captured and held with comparative ease I feel sure.
The entire detachment worked very well indeed.

THE FOLLOWING MESSAGES WERE SENT TO BRIGADE HEADQUARTERS.

C.I.Y. 1. by telephone at 5.20am.
"CIVIC". 21..7..17.
ADELPHI.
"CISTERN". 5.20am.

C.I.Y.2. by telephone at 6.30am.
"CIVIC" 31..7..17.
O.P. report BLUE LINE captured.
"CISTERN". 6.30am.

C.I.Y.3. by telephone 7.26am.
"CIVIC" 31..7..17.
Battalion moving forward. Hedaquarters moving to J.14.a.4.3.
"CISTERN" 7.26am.

D.D. message from about JACKDAW RESERVE 8am.
"Enemy holding W.edge of GLENCORSE WOOD".

D.D. message by lamp from J.13.d.8.7. at 9.25am.
"Enemy hold W.edge of GLENCORSE WOOD. Am advancing on Strong
"point J.14.a.3.3. and trench running N.E."

D.D. message by lamp from J.13.d.8.7. at 9.55am.
"Enemy hold strong point J.14.a.3.3, trench N.E. and JARGON
"TRENCH. Held up MENIN ROAD by M.G's.

C.O.1. by Battalion Runners at 11am.
"CIPHER".
The enemy are holding strongly with M.G's the following line, JAP TRENCH - JARGON TRENCH & Strong Point J.14.a.3.3. Our line at present runs about 300 yards in front of MENIN ROAD. We are in touch with Berks and 17th.K.L.R. It was impossible to advance with the barrage. Still endeavouring to capture strong points. Berks and my H.Q. under bank of MENIN ROAD about J.13.b.5.0. There was a gap between Berks and 2nd. Berks but has been filled. Stokes Mortars and ammunition required. All tanks ditched or knocked out. Estimated casualties 4 Officers 110 O.R.
Berks. ditto.
CISTERN 11am.

2.

It would probably be possible to advance if barrage put down to cover line given you held by enemy. Heavy enemy shelling 5.9. now coming from nearly due East.

C.O.2. by Brigade Runner at 12 noon.
"CIVIC"
The enemy are holding strongly with M.G's the following line JAP - JARGON TRENCH & Strong Point J.14.a.3.3. Our line at present runs about 300 yards in front of MENIN ROAD. We are in touch with Berks & 17th.K.L.R. It was impossible to advance with the barrage. Still endeavouring to capture strong points. Berks & my H.Q. under Bank of MENIN ROAD about J.13.b.5.0. Berks in touch with 2nd. Berks. Stokes mortar and ammunition required. All tanks ditched or knocked out. Estimated casualties 4 Officers 110 O.R.
Berks. ditto.
It would probably be possible to advanceif barrage put down to cover line given you held by enemy. Heavy enemy shelling 5.9. from nearly due E.
We are digging in on our present line.
"CISTERN" 12 noon.

By Cyclist Coy. from O.P. about J.13.d.8.7. and duplicated by Pigeon Message from same Coy. at 1.50pm.

"All our heavies firing short. Want strong point & W. edge of GLENCORSE WOOD Shelled. Approximate increase of range 60 yards.

C.O.3. by Brigade Runner at 3pm.
"CIVIC"
Prisoners of 1st. Bn. 238th. Regt. state 3 M.G's in strong point J.14.a.3.3 300 men in JARGON TRENCH. 3 Battalions behind them. 1 in BERCELAIRE. 1 in REUTEL. 1 just N. of that. They came up in busses from ARRAS district this morning.
"CISTERN" 3pm.

C.O.4. by Brigade Runner at 5.35pm.
"CIVIC"
Headquarters about J.13.b.3.3. Line runs approximately as follows, J.13.b.8.4. - J.14.a.0.3. - J.14.c.1.8. & are in touch on both flanks. Pigeon message was correct but line was forced to withdraw. Only a portion of Strong Point was reached & evacuated owing to casualties & no touch on right.
"CISTERN" 5.35pm.

THE FOLLOWING MESSAGES WERE RECEIVED FROM BRIGADE H.Q. AT THE TIMES STATED AT THE FOOT OF EACH.

B.M. 3. 31. CISTERN.
"BATH report BLUE LINE Taken.
"CIVIC" 6. 20am. Received 6.27am.

B.O.5. 31st. CISTERN.
"AREA report they have taken BLACK LINE.
"CIVIC" 7am. Received 7.20am.

B.O.12. 31st. CISTERN.
"Bosche assembling for counter attack in J.2.d. J.8.b. & d. If BATH have not made good BLACK LINE you will not push on until situation developes favourably. In the meantime assist BATH in making good the ground already gained."
"CIVIC" 9.10am. Received 11.45am.

B.O.14. 31st. CISTERN.
"BUCK ordered to make good BLACK LINE with its two Reserve Battns. These 2 Battns. will advance through you under a barrage Keep your Battn. as fresh as possible so that it can carry out original role of capturing GREEN LINE when BUCK has made good BLACK LINE. No orders received about barrage for BLACK LINE but your Bn. will follow in rear of BUCKS Bns. & will form up as close as possible to the BLACK LINE ready to advance as soon a the barrage intensifies. In case you do not receive Zero hour in time, warn your men that intensification of barrage is signa to advance from BLACK LINE. Your messages times 11am. & 12 noon received. Am sending up T.M. Ammunition to your H.Q. Sorry cannot send Stokes Mortar. A 6" Battery is being put on to Hun Strong Point J.14.a.3.3. Sorry about your casualties, your boys are doing alright. Another Company of Tanks had been ordered up.
"CIVIC" 12.55pm. Received 1.50pm.

B.O.16. 31st. CISTERN.
"Captured map shews enemy M.G's just S. of road at J.8.c.3.2. and at J.14.a.3½-3½. "CIVIC" 2.50pm. Received 3.35pm.

B.O.18. 31st. CISTERN.
"Report position of your H.Q. & dispositions of your Bn. especially as regards points of junction of flanks. 2 Bns. of BRACE are attacking BLACK LINE at 7pm. tonight & will move through you. Am sending up ammunition. Try & get ammunition fro direlect tanks. Attached is copy of pigeon message received. I do not think this is correct. Verify & send back word immediately as if correct must inform attacking troops. Tunnel under the YPRES-MENIN RD. is mined from I.18.b.60.45 to J.13.a.25.35. "CIVIC" 4.15pm. Received 5pm.

23rd. Bde. Order No. 09 was received at 7.20pm.

GENERAL REMARKS

1. Advance in Artillery Formation.

The advance from the forward assembly area as far as JACKDAW RESERVE was carried out in Artillery formation, There was a slight tendancy to bear too much to the left but this was corrected at JACKDAW RESERVE. The enemy barrage on SANCTUARY WOOD was very severe, & on arrival at the E. edge direct M.G. & Rifle fire was encountered from enemy on the YPRES -MENIN RD. & in the vicinity of STIRLING CASTLE.

2. The advance from JACKDAW RESERVE to the YPRES -MENIN ROAD.

It was found to be absolutely necessary to deploy on the line of JACKDAW RESERVE owing to the rifle & M.G. fire. Very few of the 90th. Bde. (30th. Div). were seen on this line. The advance was continued, good rapidity being maintained as far as the YPRES-MENIN RD. Several parties of the enemy & individual men were either shot or forced to retire from their positions by means of covering L.G. & Rifle fire. Two detachments with automatic rifles were killed on the Menin Rd. about J.13.b.4.1. The line of the YPRES-MENIN RD. was reached about 9am.

3. The advance from YPRES-MENIN RD.

From the YPRES -MENIN RD. the advance was entirely carried out by small rushes from shell hole to shell hole. owing to the heavy & accurate M.G. fire & Rifle fire from the enemy strong point J.14.a.3.3. trench running N.E. of JARGON TRENCH. The following approximate line was eventually reached & consolidation carried out as rapidly & well as possible, J.13.b.8.4. - J.14.a.0.3. - J.14.c.1.0. Heavy enemy shelling commenced about 10.45am. At about 11am. several enemy aeroplanes flew very low over our lines all round the MENIN RD. soon after this enemy shell fire from nearly due E. became still heavier. This, coupled with continual M.G. & Rifle fire made consolidation & communication of any sort extremely difficult. Practically none of the 90th. Bde. (30th. Div). were seen on the line of the YPRES-MENIN RD. Touch was continually maintained with the 6th. R. Barkshire Regt. & touch with the 17th. K.L.R. was definitely established by our most forward troops by 4pm. although prior to this (10am.) I had personally seen this Battn. located their left, & ordered an Officer to take up a more suitable position from which he could bring fire on the enemy Strong Point at J.14.a.3.3. & get in touch with "C" Coy. besides gaining possession of some high ground in his immediate front about J.14.c.2.6. along line of JASPER LANE to about J.14.c.45.30. I saw him start off to carry this out.

4. Communication.

Several D.D. signal messages were sent back but owing to very poor visibility & smoke from the enemy shell fire on SANCTUARY WOOD & forward of it few, if any were received. All forward communication had to be carried out by Runners. A list of messages sent to Bde. H.Q. & how sent is attached.

5. Medical Arrangements.

During the early stages until the bearer Coy. established their station in the MENIN RD. TUNNELL about J.13.b.2.3. little evacuation could be done beyond Battn. H.Q. By dark all the Battn. wounded were brought in by the Regimental Stretcher Bearers. I cannot speak too highly on the conduct of all bearers. The casualties among them were severe.

6. Enemy's Action.

The enemy's shell fire did not appear to be so severe until we advanced through SANCTUARY WOOD, he then, must have had direct observation as his fire was accurate & contin--ually followed the movements of our advancing troops. He appeared to act with extraordinary little cunning in the handling of his M.G's. Had he withheld fire for even a ¼ of an hour he could have dealt with each platoon in detail

6 contd. & inflicted very severe casualties, as he was occupying the YPRES-MENIN RD. with direct observation to SANCTUARY WOOD. His Infantry appeared to have little stamina for fighting once our infantry got close to him, they however used their rifles although their rifle fire on the whole was poor but M.G. Fire was accurate.

7. Action of our Infantry. I cannot speak too highly of the gallantry, keenness, determ--ination, coolness & esprit de corps displayed by all ranks of the Batta. Under very heavy shell, M.G. & Rifle fire every possible good quality was most prominently displayed. N.C.O's without hesitation took command & acted with ability, this especially applies to the Junior N.C.O's but in every case the situation was quickly appreciated & dealt with in the proper manner. The advance of the Battn. was carried out by means of covering rifle & L.G. Fire entirely, & the keenness of all ranks to get forward on every occasion was very pronounced. I am quite convinced that no opportunity of using a rifle or a L.G. was let slide & on the whole the fire was accurate.

8. Guide Patrols. The Guide Patrols sent forward as detailed in Operation Order No. 20 were unable to gain touch with the 90th. Bde. who had apparently completely lost direction. They were able to give useful information regarding the situation however for at one time they were the most advanced troops in the Battalion Area.

Lieut. Col.

Commanding 8th. Battalion The Suffolk Regiment.

SUMMARY OF CASUALTIES

Officers,	KILLED.	3.	(Lt. Chibnall. 2nd. Lt. Wheeler. and 2nd. Lieut. Savage.).
do.	WOUNDED.	4	(includes 1 still at duty).
Other Ranks.	KILLED.	38	
	WOUNDED.	120	(includes 9 still at duty).
	MISSING.	12	
TOTAL CASUALTIES.....		177	

@@

Du.

When marking up documents for copying please tick the appropriate box.

- [ ] Right hand page only
- [ ] Left hand page only
- [ ] Right hand Page start
- [ ] Left hand page start
- [ ] Right hand page stop
- [ ] Left hand page stop

Please use a separate slip for each instruction.

e.g. If copying several continuous pages you require one slip to indicate where to start copying and another slip to indicate where the copying should end.

53rd MGC.

YPRES OPERATIONS

------July 3rd. to 31st. 1917.---

July 3rd. The Battalion left the ARRAS Area by train, arrived at CASSEL at 7.30am. on the 4th. and marched to billets and bivouacs in farms about the STEENVOORDE Area.

July 4th. All Officers were addressed by the 2nd. Corps Commander - (Lieut. General JACOBS. K.C.B.) on the subject of the forthcoming operations.

July 6th. to 24th. Training of all sorts was carried out on areas and such places as were available and suitable.
Brigade, Battalion and Company Conferences were continually being held. Parties of Officers, N.C.O's and men were daily visiting the forward area, and a model of the ground near BUSSE - BOOM and were conveyed to and from by Motor Lorries.

July 25th. The Battalion was due to leave the STEENVOORDE Area at 10.45pm. this was cancelled at about 5pm.
Battalion Operation Orders for the forthcoming Operations were issued early in the morning.

July 26th. At 11.45am. the Brigadier (Brigadier-General Higginson D.S.O.) addressed the Battalion on the subject of the forthcoming operations, expressing his complete confidence in them and wishing them every possible good fortune.

July 28th. The Battalion left Billets at 10pm. and marched to a Camp at G.32.c. near RENINGHELST (Belguim, Sheet 28.1/20,000.N.W.). where it arrived at 1.30am. on the 29th.
Heavy thunderstorm at 7am. rain lasted till 12 noon.

July 29th. At 3pm. the final conference was held at Brigade Headquarters The Battalion left this Camp at 7.30pm. and marched by Companies to NEW DICKEBUSCH CAMP where it arrived at 10.30pm.

July 30th. A nice fine morning early, but this soon turned into a steady drizzle which lasted till 11am. when the rain ceased. The Battalion left this Camp by platoons for the forward Assembly Area in the following order, starting at 9.30pm. "A" Coy. "B" Coy. H.Q.Coy. "D" Coy. T.M.Battery (1 gun team) "C" Coy. half section M.G.Coy.
The Blue track which was picketed under 2nd. Lt. N. Bolingbroke by N.C.O's and men from the "Details" was followed throughout. The night was comparatively quiet as regards enemy shelling. The Battalion only suffered when "C" Coy. reached ZILLIBEKE VILLAGE.

July 31st. The whole Battalion was located in the forward assemble Area. (Details, Operation Order No.30) by 2am. At this hour and up till "Zero Hour" the enemy shell fire appreciably increased. "ZERO HOUR" was 3.50am.
At this hour the light was distinctly bad, visibility being only possible for a very short distance. From this Point onwards I will deal with Battalion Headquarters, each Company, 1 gun T.M.Battery and the half section M.G.Company in detail, finishing with a few general remarks and a list of the casualties.

B A T T A L I O N   H E A D Q U A R T E R S

At "Zero Hour" Battalion Headquarters was established in WELLINGTON CRESCENT. At 7.20am. Headquarters started to move forward with a view to establishing themselves at J.14.a.4.3. or that vicinity. A heavy enemy barrage was encountered in SANCTUARY WOOD and on the eastern edge Machine Gun and Rifle fire was met.

The first halt was made on the line of JACKDAW RESERVE where it was seen that the enemy were holding YPRES - MENIN ROAD, western edge of GLENCORSE WOOD and Strong Point J.14.a.3.3. this was at about 8.10am.

Headquarters were eventually moved up to about J.13.b.5.0. where they were established by 9.15am.

A visual signal station was established at about J.13.d.8.7. At about 2.30pm. Headquarters were moved to the Tunnell under the YPRES - MENIN ROAD, at about J.13.b.2.3.

The Battalion Scouts under Lieut.R.C.BOLINGBROKE had moved forward at 6am. to assist in marking out the route forward. As they encountered practically none of the 90th.Brigade Lieut.BOLINGBROKE decided to gain what information he could. He reached the BLUE LINE about J.13.b.6.3. where he was wounded in the head and shoulder, he remained at duty until he could do nothing further.

The work performed by Lieut.BOLINGBROKE, as on all occasions been most conspicuous, and on this occasion it was as usual marked by great gallantry, determination and disregard of everything personal in order to gain information and assist the operations.

Battalion Headquarters eventually left J.13.b.2.3. at about 4am. on Morning August 1st. arrived at the vicinity of RITZ STREET at about 5.30am. and at the Camp at DICKEBUSCHE at about 7am.

I particularly wish to place on record the gallant and admirable work performed by the following throughout these operations.

Capt. & Adjt. G.L.M.Fache. M.C.
Lieut. R.C. Bolingbroke.
3/9691. R.S.M. W. Goody.
14791. Pte. P.Leader.
14684. Pte. C.C.Arbin.
14520. Pte. W.J.Riches.

"A" COMPANY

The Company left the forward assembly area (NORMAN TRENCH) at 7am. in the following order,

Company Headqyarters.
Nos.2 and 4 Platoons 1st.Line.
No.3.Platoon 2nd.Line.
No.4.Platoon 3rd.Line.

A certain amount of loss of direction occurred at the commencement but this was eventually rectified and by the time the MENIN ROAD was reached the left of the Company was on more or less its allotted front. The frontage covered by the Coy.was not however as large as was intended but this under the corcumstances was unavoidable. The enemy's barrage was encountered in SANCTUARY WOOD & in addition M.G.Fire from GLENCORSE WOOD & the MENIN ROAD and these inflicted the first casualties on the Company. Close to the MENIN ROAD an Officer of the Manchester Regt.was metwho said that GLENCORSE WOOD was in our hands,he was one of the very few of the 90th.Brigade(30th. Division)seen throughout the day on the Battalion Frontage,his information was however soon contradicted by Lieut.BOLINGBROKE.The enemy were obviously holding much of the ground to the West of GLENCORSE WOOD. Nos.2 and 4 Platoons under 2nd.Lieut.MASTIN were now ordered to advance by sections and make good the ridge S.E. of SURBITON VILLAS,these platoons were followed by Nos.1 & 3 under 2nd.Lieut.WHEELER. Good progress was made for about 300 yards when the line was held up by M.G.Fire from the right. No.18182.Pte.READ.F. and a few other men put this gun out of action & killed the team on their own initiative & this allowed the advance to again continue to the ridge in question. Progress was however slow throughout owing to heavy M.G. & Rifle Fire which necessitated the advance being carried out from shell hole to shell hole. From this position no further progress was possible as the enemy's M.G.Fire & Rifle Fire was too heavy & accurate. An attempt was made by 2nd.Lieut.WHEELER under covering fire from the left directed by Lieut.BOLINGBROKE to advance,but casualties were too heavy,2nd.Lieut. WHEELER among others being killed in the attempt. 2 sections of No.4. Platoon further to the right with "C" Coy.were able to push forward but these were later forced to withdraw owing to our own heavies firing short. Four Tanks now made their appearance and made most gallant attempts to get forward,they were all in turn knocked out by heavy enemy shell fire directed against them. It was now decided to dig in and consolidate as well as possible the ground gained,but this work was much hindered by M.G. & shell fire. The latter becoming both accurate & severe after enemy areoplanes flying low had reconnoitred our positions. All these planes were heavily fired on by rifles,L.G. & M.G'S but were not apparently brought down. At about 8.30pm.orders as to the relief by the 19th. K.L.R. were received & the Coy.eventually moved back at midnight. During the whole of these operations the behaviour of all ranks was throughout beyond praise. Officers & N.C.O's grasped the situation & acted with promptness,judgement & determination. The features of the ground were made good use of & every opportunity of inflicting to the enemy & assisting the advance by rifle fire was seized. I particularly wish to place on record the gallant & valuable work per formed throughout by the following:-

Capt.H.A.Angier.M.C. 2nd.Lt.J.D.Wheeler(Killed) 2nd.Lt.S.L.A.Mastin.
3/9732.C.S.M.D.Wells. 3/9686.Sgt.T.Eaves. 14174.Sgt.C.Smith.
12882.Cpl.H.J.Westley. 18182.Pte.F.Read. 13986.Pte.S.G.Smith.
14050.Pte.J.Lucas. 14478. Pte.O.Rainsford(Killed).

"B" COMPANY.

The Company started its advance in artillery formation from the forward assembly area at 7.45am.

Heavy enemy shell fire was encountered in SANCTUARY WOOD and at the Eastern edge some machine gun fire, the line of JACKDAW RESERVE was reached with very little loss.

From here it was found quite necessary to deploy & move by sections, the section Commanders in every case took command and lead their sections with ability and confidence.

On reaching the vicinity of SURBITON VILLAS fighting became particularly heavy, casualties occuring frequently from the enemy M.G. and rifle fire.

All sections and particularly the Lewis Guns from this point did very good work against the enemy, the covering fire was accurate, well directed and controlled. The advance onwards was purely a matter of rushes, chiefly from shell hole to shell hole, touch was maintained right and left throughout & eventually the line was forced to halt about 200 yards East of SURBITON VILLAS. It was during this advance that Lieut. R.S. CHIBNALL was killed. This line was held till about 2pm. when, through heavy enemy shelling & our own heavies firing short it was forced to withdraw with the left in touch with the 6th. Royal Berkshire Regt. at about J.13.b.8.4. I cannot speak too highly of the keenness, determination, pluck, and gallantry displayed by all ranks of the Company during a very severe and hard fought action.

The relief of the Coy. was completed by about 1am. August 1st.

I particularly wish to place on record the valuable work performed by the following.

Capt. E.J. Greene. M.C.
Lieut. R.S. Chibnall. (Killed).
2nd. Lieut. L.P. Pells.
2nd. Lieut. G.G. Hannan.
3/9662. Sgt. A.E. Norris.
3/10115. Sgt. G.W. Pooley.
15401. Sgt. C. Brookes.
16103. Cpl. W.G. Batchelor.
18014. L/C. A.W. Wright.
25008. L/C. H. Impey.
40442. L/C. J. Osborne.
14688. L/C., G.H. Mayes.
14103. L/C. W. Davey.
14971. Pte. H. Doy.

"C" COMPANY.

The Coy. unfortunately lost 5 men killed & 3 wounded in addition to 1 Lewis Gun in ZILLIBEKE on the way up to the forward assembly area on night of 30th. At 7.10am. the Coy. formed up in Artillery formation and left the assembly trenches about 150 yards behind the support Coy. at 7.20am. Through SANCTUARY WOOD the enemy barrage was very heavy & the M.G. fire on the Eastern Edge was distinctly heavy. Platoon Commanders shewed good judgement during this advance in the observation of the enemy shell fire. On arrival at the MENIN ROAD the entire frantage of the Battalion was not occupied & it was found necessary to prolong the line to the right in order to, both occupy our frontage & gain touch with the 17th. K.L.R. on our right. No one of the 90th. Brigade (30th. Division) was met during the advance of the Company up to and beyond the MENIN ROAD, the only information obtainable was from our own observation & 2nd. Lt. Hannan (Patrol Guide), who was met on the MENIN ROAD. Progress beyond the MENIN ROAD was held up by M.G. fire & rifle fire from the strong point J.14.a.3.3. until one Stokes Gun was brought into action. Under cover from this & fire from the M.G. attached to the Battalion & rifle fire the Coy. was able to push forward. The advance to JAP AVENUE was successfully accomplished & here a temporary halt was necessary. Rifle and L.G. fire together with rifle grenades were now directed against the enemy strong point & on a trench in the Sunken Road (J.14.a). & when the situation appeared favourable a further advance to within 100 yards of the strong point was carried out. From here it was not possible to advance further & consolidation of shell holes was commenced, this was very considerably hampered by M.G. & Rifle Fire from the strong point J.14.a.3.3. GLENCORSE WOOD and INVERNESS COPSE. The Coy. was not now in touch with the 17th. K.L.R. on the right although our right flank was even over our boundary line. The position did not appear at all satisfactory & Lieut. Srgles decided to make an attempt to rush the strong point & thus strengthen the whole position. The attempt was partially successful, a footing was gained, 1 M.G. put out of action & 20 prisoners taken & a considerable number of the enemy killed. The Company on the left were not able to advance however & owing to this in addition to heavy enemy shell, M.G. & T.M. fire the line withdrew to its original position. Our own heavies were now falling short & coupled with the accurate & heavy enemy shelling directed by low flying aeroplanes made our position very uncomfortable & in fact absolutely untenable, & the line had to be still further withdrawn to JAP AVENUE where touch was now gained with the 17th. K.L.R. on the right. The Coy. was eventually relieved by the 19th. K.L.R. early on morning of August 1st. The fine spirit, unerring devotion to duty & determination to push on & give every assistance to other units in the face of very heavy fire, displayed by all ranks of this Coy. deserves the highest praise. The Coy. lost 1 Officer Killed (2nd. Lt. Savage), 1 Officer wounded (2nd. Lt. Rae) who however remained at duty throughout, & 5 Sgts. & I cannot speak too highly of 2nd. Lt. Argles, Commanding the Coy. & the junior N.C.O's who so ably filled the breach caused by senior casualties. It is exceedingly hard to single out individuals from a Coy. which did such magnificient work but the valuable services performed by the following are unquestionable.

2nd. Lt. C.A.C. Argles. 2nd. Lt. L.C. Rae. 2nd. Lt. A.C. Savage. (Killed).
14136. Sgt. A. Woollner. 14653. Sgt. H.J. Remblance.
13883. Sgt. E.S. Houghton. 14605. Cpl. J. Crompton.
18558. Cpl. F. Bowers. 22410. Pte. A. Champion.
16013. Pte. A. Elmer.

"D" COMPANY.

This Coy. was in support for the attack. It left the assembly trenches in artillery formation at 7.15am. In passing through SANCTUARY WOOD heavy enemy shell fire was encountered & the Coy. suffered numerous casualties. The line of the MENIN ROAD was reached about 8.45am.& up to this time practically no one of the 90th.Brigade(30th.Division) had been seen & the only information obtainable was from our own observation & our own guides who had preceded the Battalion. The Coy. was used to prolong to the right of "A" Coy.& kept touch with "C" Coy.on the right.The advance from the MENIN ROAD had to be carried out by rushes from shell hole to shell hole each advance assisted by covering rifle & L.G.Fire.The enemy's M.G. & rifle fire from the strong point at J.14.a.3.3.the trench running N.E.& JARGON TRENCH was both heavy & accurate & inflicted severe casualties & made the advance very slow.A line about 150 yards beyond the MENIN ROAD was reached & here Capt.Crandon was wounded,also 2nd.Lt.Brown,the latter however remained at duty with the Coy. throughout the operations & was executed after arrival in Camp on August 1st.The advance was continued slowly until it was found impossible in spite of many gallant attempts to continue owing to the very heavy M.G. & Rifle fire from the Strong Point & GLENCORSE WOOD. Touch was gained right & left & the work of consolidation was commenced on about the line J.13.b.9.2. - J.14.a.1.0. This work was by no means easy & the difficulties multiplied by the heavy M.G.fire & later by heavy & accurate shell fire directed by low flying hostile aeroplanes. Later on our heavies commenced to shell presumably the strong point ,out their range was considerably short. The Coy.was eventually relieved by the 19th.K.L.R.& left ~~the~~ at 2am.on morning of August 1st. The work performed by all ranks of the Coy.under most diffivult conditions was carried out with the utmost gallantry & determination.All ranks displayed the greatest keenness to get forward & if possible get to a position from which the Battalions allotted task could be carried out.

In placing on record the spelndid work of the following I only mention a very small proportion of the Coy.all of whom did most valuable work.

Capt.G.L.Crandon.M.C. who,although wounded remained at duty until he could do nothing further.

2nd.Lt.W.Brown.
2nd.Lt.F.C.J.Latham.
3/10273.Sgt.C.F.Tuttle.
6109.Sgt.P.Farrold.
15020.Sgt.C.K.Spindler.
3/10100.Cpl.T.Making.
14821.Cpl.E.J.Hazelwood.
14961.L/C.A.King.
3/9873.Pte.C.A.Wentworth.
15372.Pte.J.Sawyer.
13917.Pte.G.A.Long.
41076.Pte.C.W.Cox.
41088.Pte.A.Doodenham.
18303.Pte.H.T.Pollard.

Half Section 53rd. MACHINE GUN COMPANY.

This section under Lieut. J.C. Biggs. M.C. advanced from the assembly area with "C" Companyat 9125am. it was brought into action from about J.13.d.7.9. against the enemy strong point at J.14.a.3.3 It subsequently moved forward and was established about J.14.c.1.8. I particularly wish to draw attention to the excellent work done by Lieut. Biggs. He not only handled the half section throughout with the greatest ability, energy and determination under heavy shell, Machine Gun and rifle fire but himself worked an enemy mortar against the strong point with good effect.

---

1 Gun 53rd. TRENCH MORTAR BATTERY.

This gun under 2nd. Lt. H.S. walters and 14110. Cpl. E. Nunn advanced with the Headquarters of "D" Company.
4 carriers were lost on the advance to the MENIN ROAD and they arrived with only about 15 shells.
The gun was ably handled and brought into action at about 9.25am. from about J.13.d.0.0. against the strong point at J.14.a.3.3.
It dealt with this very effectively was the range was accurately obtained and must have inflicted numerous casualties, as the enemy were seen to be obviously shaken and disorganized while the shells were available. With an adequate supply of shells for this gun the strong point could have been captured and held with comparative ease I feel sure.
The entire detachment worked very well indeed.

THE FOLLOWING MESSAGES WERE SENT TO BRIGADE HEADQUARTERS.

C.I.Y. 1. by telephone at 5.20am.
"CIVIC". 21..7..17.
ADELPHI.
"CISTERN". 5.20am.

C.I.Y.2. by telephone at 6.30am.
"CIVIC" 31..7..17.
O.P. report BLUE LINE captured.
"CISTERN". 6.30am.

C.I.Y.3. by telephone 7.26am.
"CIVIC" 31..7..17.
Battalion moving forward. Hedaquarters moving to J.14.a.4.3.
"CISTERN" 7.26am.

D.D.message from about JACKDAW RESERVE 8am.
"Enemy holding W.edge of GLENCORSE WOOD".

D.D.message by lamp from J.13.d.8.7. at 9.25am.
"Enemy hold W.edge of GLENCORSE WOOD. Am advancing on Strong "point J.14.a.3.3. and trench running N.E."

D.D.message by lamp from J.13.d.8.7. at 9.55am.
"Enemy hold strong point J.14.a.3.3, trench N.E. and JARGON "TRENCH. Held up MENIN ROAD by M.G's.

C.O.1. by Battalion Runners at 11am.
"CIPHER".
The enemy are holding strongly with M.G's the following line, JAP TRENCH - JARGON TRENCH & Strong Point J.14.a.3.3. Our line at present runs about 300 yards in front of MENIN ROAD. We are in touch with Berks and 17th.K.L.R. It was impossible to advance with the barrage. Still endeavouring to capture strong points. Berks and my H.Q. under bank of MENIN ROAD about J.13.b.5.0. There was a gap between Berks and 2nd. Berks but has been filled. Stokes Mortars and ammunition required. All tanks ditched or knocked out. Estimated casualties 4 Officers 110 O.R.
Berks. ditto.
CISTERN 11am.

2.

It would probably be possible to advance if barrage put down to cover line given you held by enemy. Heavy enemy shelling 5.9. now coming from nearly due East.

C.O.2. by Brigade Runner at 12 noon.
"CIVIC"
The enemy are holding strongly with M.G's the following line JAP -JARGON TRENCH & Strong Point J.14.a.3.3. Our line at present runs about 300 yards in front of MENIN ROAD. We are in touch with Berks & 17th.K.L.R. It was impossible to advance with the barrage. Still endeavouring to capture strong points. Berks & my H.Q. under Bank of MENIN ROAD about J.13.b.5.0. Berks in touch with 2nd. Berks. Stokes mortar and ammunition required. All tanks ditched or knocked out. Estimated casualties 4 Officers 110 O.R.
Berks. ditto.
It would probably be possible to advanceif barrage put down to cover line given you held by enemy. Heavy enemy shelling 5.9. from nearly due E.
We are digging in on our present line.
"CISTERN" 12 noon.

By Cyclist Coy. from O.P. about J.13.d.8.7. and duplicated by Pigeon Message from same Coy. at 1.50pm.

"All our heavies firing short. Want strong point & W. edge of GLENCORSE WOOD Shelled. Approximate increase of range 60 yards.

C.O.3. by Brigade Runner at 3pm.
"CIVIC"
Prisoners of 1st. Bn. 238th. Regt. state 3 M.G's in strong point J.14.a.3.3 300 men in JARGON TRENCH. 3 Battalions behind them. 1 in BERCELAIRE. 1 in REUTEL. 1 just N. of that.
They came up in busses from ARRAS district this morning.
"CISTERN" 3pm.

C.O.4. by Brigade Runner at 5.35pm.
"CIVIC"
Headquarters about J.13.b.3.3. Line runs approximately as follows, J.13.b.8.4. - J.14.a.0.3.-J.14.c.1.8. & are in touch on both flanks. Pigeon message was correct but line was forced to withdraw. Only a portion of Strong Point was reached & evacuated owing to casualties & no touch on right.
"CISTERN" 5.35pm.

THE FOLLOWING MESSAGES WERE RECEIVED FROM BRIGADE H.Q. AT THE TIMES STATED AT THE FOOT OF EACH.

B.M. 3. 31. CISTERN.
"BATH report BLUE LINE Taken.
"CIVIC" 6. 20am. Received 6.27am.

B.O.5. 31st. CISTERN.
"AREA report they have taken BLACK LINE.
"CIVIC" 7am. Received 7.20am.

B.O.12. 31st. CISTERN.
"Bosche assembling for counter attack in J.2.d.J.8.b.& d. If BATH have not made good BLACK LINE you will not push on until situation developes favourably. In the meantime assist BATH in making good the ground already gained."
"CIVIC" 9.10am. Received 11.45am.

B.O.14. 31st. CISTERN.
"BUCK ordered to make good BLACK LINE with its two Reserve Battns. These 2 Battns. will advance through you under a barrage, Keep your Battn. as fresh as possible so that it can carry out original role of capturing GREEN LINE when BUCK has made good BLACK LINE. No orders received about barrage for BLACK LINE but your Bn. will follow in rear of BUCKS Bns. & will form up as close as possible to the BLACK LINE ready to advance as soon as the barrage intensifies. In case you do not receive Zero hour in time, warn your men that intensification of barrage is signal to advance from BLACK LINE. Your messages times 11am. & 12 noon received. Am sending up T.M. Ammunition to your H.Q. Sorry cannot send Stokes Mortar. A 6" Battery is being put on to Hun Strong Point J.14.a.3.3. Sorry about your casualties, your boys are doing alright. Another Company of Tanks had been ordered up.
"CIVIC" 12.55pm. Received 1.50pm.

B.O.16. 31st. CISTERN.
"Captured map shews enemy M.G's just S. of road at J.8.c.3.2. and at J.14.a.3½.3½. "CIVIC" 2.50pm. Received 3.35pm.

B.O.18. 31st. CISTERN.
"Report position of your H.Q. & dispositions of your Bn. especially as regards points of junction of flanks. 2 Bns. of BRACE are attacking BLACK LINE at 7pm. tonight & will move through you. Am sending up ammunition. Try & get ammunition from direlect tanks. Attached is copy of pigeon message received. I do not think this is correct. Verify & send back word immediately as if correct must inform attacking troops. Tunnell under the YPRES-MENIN RD. is mined from I.18.b.60.45 to J.13.a.25.35. "CIVIC" 4.15pm. Received 5pm.
23rd. Bde. Order No. 09 was received at 7.20pm.

GENERAL REMARKS

1. Advance in Artillery Formation.

The advance from the forward assembly area as far as JACKDAW RESERVE was carried out in Artillery formation, There was a slight tendancy to bear too much to the left but this was corrected at JACKDAW RESERVE. The enemy barrage on SANCTUARY WOOD was very severe, & on arrival at the E. edge direct M.G. & Rifle fire was encountered from enemy on the YPRES -MENIN RD. & in the vicinity of STIRLING CASTLE.

2. The advance from JACKDAW RESERVE to the YPRES -MENIN ROAD.

It was found to be absolutely necessary to deploy on the line of JACKDAW RESERVE owing to the rifle & M.G. fire. Very few of the 90th. Bde. (30th. Div). were seen on this line. The advance was continued, good rapidity being maintained as far as the YPRES-MENIN RD. Several parties of the enemy & individual men were either shot or forced to retire from their positions by means of covering L.G. & Rifle fire. Two detachments with automatic rifles were killed on the Menin Rd. about J.13.b.4.1. The line of the YPRES-MENIN RD. was reached about 9am.

3. The advance from YPRES-MENIN RD.

From the YPRES -MENIN RD. the advance was entirely carried out by small rushes from shell hole to shell hole. owing to the heavy & accurate M.G. fire & Rifle fire from the enemy strong point J.14.a.3.3. trench running N.E. of JARGON TRENCH. The following approximate line was eventually reached & consolidation carried out as rapidly & well as possible, J.13.b.8.4. - J.14.a.0.3. - J.14.c.1.0. Heavy enemy shelling commenced about 10.45am. At about 11am. several enemy aeroplanes flew very low over our lines all round the MENIN RD. soon after this enemy shell fire from nearly due E. became still heavier. This, coupled with continual M.G. & Rifle fire made consolidation & communication of any sort extremely difficult. Practically none of the 90th. Bde. (30th. Div). were seen on the line of the YPRES-MENIN RD. Touch was continually maintained with the 6th. R. Barkshire Regt. & touch with the 17th. K.L.R. was definitely established by our most forward troops by 4pm. although prior to this (10am.) I had personally seen this Battn. located their left, & ordered an Officer to take up a more suitable position from which he could bring fire on the enemy Strong Point at J.14.a.3.3. & get in touch with "C" Coy. besides gaining possession of some high ground in his immediate front about J.14.c.2.6. along line of JASPER LANE to about J.14.c.45.50. I saw him start off to carry this out.

4. Communication.

Several D.D. signal messages were sent back but owing to very poor visibility & smoke from the enemy shell fire on SANCTUARY WOOD & forward of it few, if any were received. All forward communication had to be carried out by Runners. A list of messages sent to Bde. H.Q. & how sent is attached.

5. Medical Arrangements.

During the early stages until the bearer Coy. established their station in the MENIN RD. TUNNELL about J.13.b.2.3. little evacuation could be done beyond Battn. H.Q. By dark all the Battn. wounded were brought in by the Regimental Stretcher Nearers. I cannot speak too highly on the conduct of all bearers. The casualties among them were severe.

6. Enemy's Action.

The enemy's shell fire did not appear to be so severe until we advanced through SANCTUARY WOOD, he then, must have had direct observation as his fire was accurate & contin- -ually followed the movements of our advancing troops. He appeared to act with extraordinary little cunning in the handling of his M.G's. Had he withheld fire for even a ¼ of an hour he could have dealt with each platoon in detail

6 contd. & inflicted very severe casualties, as he was occupying the YPRES-MENIN RD. with direct observation to SANCTUARY WOOD. His Infantry appeared to have little stamina for fighting once our infantry got close to him, they however used their rifles although their rifle fire on the whole was poor but M.G. Fire was accurate.

7. Action of our Infantry. I cannot speak too highly of the gallantry, keenness, determ--ination, coolness & esprit de corps displayed by all ranks of the Battn. Under very heavy shell, M.G. & Rifle fire every possible good quality was most prominently displayed. N.C.O's without hesitation took command & acted with ability, this especially applies to the Junior N.C.O's but in every case the situation was quickly appreciated & dealt with in the proper manner. The advance of the Battn. was carried out by means of covering rifle & L.G. Fire entirely, & the keenness of all ranks to get forward on every occasion was very pronounced. I am quite convinced that no opportunity of using a rifle or a L.G. was let slide & on the whole the fire was accurate.

8. Guide Patrols. The Guide Patrols sent forward as detailed in Operation Order No.20 were unable to gain touch with the 90th. Bde. who had apparently completely lost direction. They were able to give useful information regarding the situation however for at one time they were the most advanced troops in the Battalion Area.

Lieut. Col.

Commanding 8th. Battalion The Suffolk Regiment.

SUMMARY OF CASUALTIES

Officers, KILLED.	3.	(Lt. Chibnall. 2nd. Lt. Wheeler. and 2nd. Lieut. Savage.).
do. WOUNDED.	4	(includes 1 still at duty).
Other Ranks. KILLED.	38	
WOUNDED.	120	(includes 9 still at duty).
MISSING.	12	
TOTAL CASUALTIES.....	177	

Appendix A

No. 3 Section attached Infantry

Movement

2 Guns (Lt Evans) and 2 guns (Lt Briggs) to report to 6th R. Berks and 8th Suffolk respectively on Y day at New Dickebusch Camp, hour to be notified later, and move forward with these Battns.

Time Table for Guidance

Formed up in forward Assembly	By	Z + 4.15 hours
Move forward from "	"	Z + 4.15 "
Halt BLUE LINE for rest & reorganisation		Z + 5.30 "
Deploy for Assault on GREEN LINE just in rear of BLACK LINE BARRAGE OPENS		Z + 6½ hours

ORDERS

(a) Guns will be under command of O.C. Battns

(b) Sections will assimilate as nearly as possible the Infantry

(c) During the advance most strict attention must be paid to FIRE CONTROL should targets be available. The depth of the advance calls for the maximum amount of ammunition reaching the final positions.

Allocation of Loads.

(9 Infantry men will be attached to each gun)

Sgt or Cpl. 100 rounds in bandolier, condenser tube and bag 1 Very pistol 6 rounds V.P.A white and 6 S.O.S.

No. 1. Tripod
2. Gun and Spare parts
3. 2 Petrol Cans water
4. 2 Belt Boxes
5. 2 "

No. 6. 1 Belt Box 500 rounds SAA
7. —do—
8. —do—
9. —do—

Mills Bombs.

Arrangements are being made for a supply of Mills Bombs to be carried

Rations

Sections attached to Battns will be rationed through Battalions.

Guns

The Brigade Commander will probably take over the guns of 54th M.G. Coy

Appendix D

Transport:

a) Will be brigaded 1/2 night and 2 day at Neu [illegible]ROBUSCH Camp (H33 a [illegible])

b) Divisional Train

Undernoted will report to the Divisional Train (Park) at [illegible]

1/Lt S. S. O. R. E.

1 Lt Carver

7 Drivers
7 Horses
1 2 Co
1 { Cooks / Batman. }

c) Rations and water up to and including 2 days to be taken. Picketing gear, Nose bags & Camp Kettle.

Secret

O.O. No. 3
Copy No. 3

53rd Machine Gun Company

ZILLEBEKE 1/10000 Ed. 5a
C-10/P12 1/20000 Ed 1.

In the Field
July 25th 19[illegible]

Information 1. (a) The II Corps in conjunction with other Corps and its right and left will attack the enemy in front of it on "Z" day
(b) The II Corps will attack as follows:—
The [illegible] Division on the right
" [illegible] " supported by the 18th Division in centre.
" [illegible] " supported by [illegible] 25th Division on the left.
(c) Attack of [illegible] Division on BLACK LINE will be carried out by the 21st Inf Bde on the right and 90th Inf Bde on left. [illegible] Inf Bde on the GREEN LINE [illegible] by the 20th K.L.R on the right and the 17th K.L.R on the left. These battns will pass through the troops which [illegible] captured the BLACK LINE
(d) The attack of the 8th Division on the GREEN [illegible] will be carried out by the 25th Inf Bde the 2nd [illegible] R. being on the right
(e) The attack of the 18th Division on the GREEN and RED LINES will be carried out by the 53rd Inf Bde (supported by the [illegible] Bde) and will pass through the [illegible] troops [illegible]
(f) 1 Sec. [illegible] (?) will co-operate with the 53rd Inf Bde in the attack

Objectives (2) The general lines of the objectives of [illegible] of the 53rd Inf Bde and [illegible] [illegible] shown on Map [illegible]

[illegible] of M G Coy (3)

See Appendix "A"

(a) No 3 Section will be attached to the assaulting batns.
2 guns (Lt Heggs) will come under command of O.C. 7th SUFFOLK REGT.
2 guns (Lt Evans) will come under command of O.C. 6th R. BERKS REGT.

See Appendix "B"

(b) No 4 Section will be attached to 8th NORFOLK R for consolidation.
2 guns (Lt Baxter) one each will garrison B & D Strong Points
2 guns (2/Lt Allen) one each will garrison A & C Strong Points

See Appendix "C"

(c) Nos 1 & 2 Section (Lt Chester & 2/Lt Leith) will come under command of D.M.G.O for Barrage Work.
Locations
2/Lt Newton will command attached carrying party for these guns

Dress

(4) Fighting Order, Haversack on back. Respirators "Alert". Rations for "Z" day & an Iron Ration. Water bottles full at Zero plus 2 hours. Officers dressed same as men. Sticks not to be carried.

Locations Y-Z Night

(5) No 3 Section - Kitz Street Area
No 4 " - Head of Kneewater [illegible]
No 1 & 2 - Barrage Positions

Dumps

(6) Div Bomb Store H 26 c 9.1 [illegible]
Adv. " " [illegible]
Brigade Dump [illegible] 80 000 SAA
" " J 8 b 1.0 35 000 SAA
" " J 9 c 0.4 35 000 SAA

Communication

7. (5) [illegible] Rockets
upon arriving [illegible]
[illegible]
[illegible]
[illegible]
[illegible]
[illegible]
[illegible]
[illegible]
[illegible]

Situation Report

(6) Special message forms with
map printed on them will be
used [illegible] to be sent
every 2 hours [illegible] where
infantry are not already using this

Maps

(7) All spare copies of maps [illegible]
[illegible] only. No additional
information is to be entered on
these maps.

Medical arrangements

(8)
S.C. 137 [illegible]
Bearer Div of 86 Fd Amb will accompany
Brigade.
Adv. Dressing Stn within [illegible]

Transport Arrangements

(1) Appendix "D"

Head quarters

(2) Bde HQ prior to zero
and during [illegible] C92
[illegible] BHQ [illegible] 59
On capture of Red Green line [illegible]
BHQ will be established about [illegible]
and on satisfactory [illegible]
communication with [illegible] being
established HQ at [illegible] 59 will be
closed.

H Q (Continued)

H Q H Q will be no [illegible] and [illegible] move forward with [illegible] B[illegible] H[illegible]

Assaulting Btts
{ Prior to Zero — RITZ Street AREA
{ Zero + — 6 Suffs. T14c 4 — 2 Berks T14a 6.6
{ After Capture of Green line [illegible] T9 0.3 Suffs — T9c.44 Berks

ESSEX REGT
{ Till Zero — 3 [illegible] Dugouts (T.21 G
{ Thence to RITZ Street Area

NORFOLK REGT
{ Prior to Zero — CRATER [illegible]
{ [illegible] — LILLEBONE [illegible]

Syncronization of Watches (13) Watches will be Synchronized at

Zero (14) To be notified later

[illegible] (15)

[illegible] Capt

[illegible] of O.O.s. to —
O.C. Coy
[illegible]
War Diary
" "
" "
O.C. No 1 Sec
" 2 "
" 3 "
" 4 "
B.M.G.O.
[illegible]
12 Brigade
12/16 Battns.

[illegible]
[illegible]

[illegible]

General. Guns will report to [illegible] of 5th [illegible] at [illegible] [illegible] from where they will move forward [illegible]. Route to be notified later.

To No 1 Platoon Strong Point "A"
Commanded by Lt D.D. Lee 5th [illegible]
Assembles Norman Str [illegible]

To No 2 Platoon Strong Point "B"
Commanded by Lt A. Holmes RE
Assembles Kitz Str L + 4 [illegible]

To No 3 Platoon Strong Point "C"
Commanded by Lt C.T. Blackburn
Assembles Norman Str L + 4 15

To No 4 Platoon Strong Point "D"
Commanded by Lt Pickering RE
Assembles Kitz Str L + 4 [illegible]

Orders Guns will assist consolidation work and on completion move so they can best assist their defence. Posts will be held to the last and no guns will be withdrawn without written orders from Bde HQ.

Allocation of loads. (1 infantry man will be attached to each gun team)

Sgt or Cpl 100 rounds S.A.A., condenser tube and bag, [illegible] rounds [illegible]
[illegible] [illegible], ammunition and 4 S.O.S.

No 1. Tripod — No 6 [illegible]
2. Gun and [illegible] part — 7 "
3. [illegible] water — 8 "
4. [illegible] box — 9 "
5. "

Rations Sections attached to Battns will be rationed through the Battns.

General The Brigade Commander will probably have [illegible] on guns of 5th M.G. Coy.

[illegible] OPERATIONS [illegible]

[illegible] (? [illegible])

[illegible] HONDEGHEM [illegible] CAME [illegible] by

A [illegible] positions in MAPLE TRENCH.
[illegible] under [illegible] of SANCTUARY
CORNER [illegible] for [illegible] and

[illegible] JONES wounded [illegible]
[illegible] road.
[illegible] extricated with
difficulty [illegible] NUNN & PHILLIPS [illegible]
[illegible]
[illegible] attack [illegible]

[illegible] ZILLEBEKE & [illegible]
proceeded to MAPLE TRENCH [illegible]
reached at dawn [illegible]

[illegible] CHENERY [illegible]
[illegible] forward.

[illegible]
[illegible]
[illegible] MAPLE TRENCH.
[illegible]
D.M.G.O.

[illegible] fire [illegible]
[illegible]
[illegible] immediate front.

[illegible] expended 35,000 rounds.

[illegible] A [illegible] position + 2 [illegible] quiet

till SANCTUARY WOOD was [illegible] Came
under M.G. fire from direction of

STIRLING CASTLE [illegible] BROWN [illegible]
SANCTUARY WOOD
CLAPHAM JUNCTION [illegible] [illegible] heavy casualties.
Lt WEBB was found [illegible] [illegible] [illegible] wounded.
Eventually CHATEAU WOOD [illegible] [illegible] [illegible] to the [illegible] TUNNEL.
Lt SHOTTER went forward & found our line [illegible] the TARGON SWITCH and DRIVE the enemy holding TARGON TRENCH.
Lt SHOTTER then handed a report to be [illegible] through an artillery line. [illegible] found [illegible] to be cut & the message [illegible] come through.
During the afternoon Lt SHOTTER [illegible] counter attack was repulsed from GLENCORSE WOOD. [illegible] [illegible] defensive line [illegible] the repulsed attack.
[illegible] [illegible] in accordance with orders.

Total casualties

[illegible] wounded
1 O.R. missing
1 O.R. gassed.

CONSOLIDATION GUNS (No 4 [illegible])
[illegible] to 1st NORFOLKS & [illegible]
with them to ZILLEBEKE BUND

No 1 Tank A Strong Point No 7 Platoon
" 2 " B " " No 11 "
" 3 " C " " No 8 "
" 4 " D " " No 14 "

[illegible] to TANLEY STREET Nos 1 3 &
4 tanks got [illegible] & await further
orders

No 2 Tank left TANLEY STREET at 10 am
with No 11 Platoon. It was found impossible
to keep up with the infantry the tank
therefore proceeded independently.
They [illegible] too far left & got into [illegible]
[illegible] Here information was given that all
objectives had been taken. The tank then
[illegible] to B strong point & came
under heavy MG fire from this point.
It was then discovered our objectives had
not been taken the gun was withdrawn
& finally took up a position in TARGON
SWITCH where it was hit by shell fire & put
out of action.
At dusk the team withdrew & proceeded
back to ZILLEBEKE BUND.

11

Casualties:

ASSAULT GUNS.

Attached Party.

The two guns moved through to PTL STREET area & opposite Cpl AHHUBSEN bridge. Company were then attached during [illegible] position.

[illegible] moved forward from PTL at [illegible] [illegible] until EVAN [illegible] the guns when they were caught in a heavy barrage in SANCTUARY WOOD. Rest of the ranks became casualties & all [illegible] became casualties.

The remainder of the two guns had moved forward under Sgt HALL crossed the main YPRES–MENIN road into CHATEAU WOOD where they were unable to go further from heavy shelling.

The other section of the guns proceeded along road running out of CHATEAU WOOD. By this time all touch with BERKS had been lost and [illegible] Sgt HALL & 3 ORs became casualties.

From this point LIEUT HITCHINSON

took command of the two guns & the 5 O.R. unwounded. They proceeded along the road & came into action in the neighbourhood of TARGON SWITCH.

There was a party in the position of 3 Lewis Guns R.E., ESSEX, BERKS & NORFOLKS.

Several parties of Huns coming over the open into TARGON TRENCH were engaged with excellent effect.

The guns remained in position until the whole party was relieved by the KINGS LIVERPOOL.

L/Cpl HUTCHINSON was successful in bringing back to FITZ STREET two guns & two tripods complete.

The action of the junior N.C.O. & the 5 O.R. with him could not have been excelled.

Attached SUFFOLKS ([illegible] action [illegible] guns)

[illegible] C Coy in FITZ STREET went forward with the [illegible] about 7.20 am [illegible] MILLER House [illegible] SANCTUARY WOOD.

Reached the [illegible] along the YPRES MENIN road by CLAPHAM JUNCTION shortly after the infantry whom we found held up by rifle & M.G. fire from JARGON DRIVE immediately in front. One gun was brought into action here on N. side of road & assisted by Lewis Guns swept the Hun parapet & communication trenches. Enemy's fire was lessened.

Five minutes later the second gun came into action & the pair were pushed forward to parados of JAP AVENUE.

Enemy's fire was now overcome & under cover of the protective fire from these & the Lewis Guns our infantry pushed forward some 200 yards.

Trouble was still encountered from JARGON DRIVE & the immediate front.

Lt BIGGS here found a Boche anti Tank Gun (2½"-3") with revolving turret.

Lt BIGGS cleared the gun of an obstruction & after a short trial opened fire with it on the strong point. Several direct hits were obtained & shortly afterwards six Huns were seen to surrender from this point to a SUFFOLK officer. The strong point was entered by the SUFFOLKS but owing to strength of the enemy on their left were unable to hold it.

Some 60 rounds were fired from this Hun gun.

Our M.G's had meantime kept up

7

intermittent fire on enemys line.
Guns were withdrawn at 10 pm.
4 O.R. becoming casualties during the withdrawal.

Note

Owing to the heavy going the greatest difficulty was experienced in keeping up with the infantry in almost every case.

[illegible] Capt
53rd M.G. Coy.

Ref. ZILLEBEKE 1/10,000

16

53 M G Coy
18th Divn

Vol 18

Army Form C. 2118.

WAR DIARY
or
~~INTELLIGENCE SUMMARY.~~
(Erase heading not required.)

Instructions regarding War Diaries and Intelligence Summaries are contained in F. S. Regs., Part II. and the Staff Manual respectively. Title pages will be prepared in manuscript.

Place	Date	Hour	Summary of Events and Information	Remarks and references to Appendices
YPRES. OPERATIONS	1/8/17		Coy was relieved in the line on 31 July 1st Aug & moved back to DICKEBUSCH HUTS 4. 30 am. 1st Aug.	
			Evening of same day moved to OTTAWA CAMP RAINING	
	2/8/17		Spent in drying men's clothes.	
	3/8/17		"D°" & cleaning guns & material.	
	4/8/17		Moved to DICKEBUSCH HUTS	
	5/8/17		Sunday.	
	6/8/17		Coy training and refitting	
	7/8/17		"D°"	
	8/8/17		3 sections moved to MAPLE TRENCH I24 a 25.48 to carry out BARRAGE on the following morning in support of 54th & 55th Bdes - assaulting	
	9/8/17		Moved back to DICKEBUSCH as operations were postponed. Ordered same evening to move again to MAPLE TRENCH	
	10/8/17		3 Sections carried out BARRAGE PROGRAMME (see appendix "A") and moved back in the afternoon to DICKEBUSCH HUTS	Appendix Barrage Map [illegible]

[illegible] Lieut
a/O.C. 53 M.G.C.

A5834 Wt. W4973/M687 750,000 8/16 D. D. & L. Ltd. Forms/C.2118/13.

Maps. ZILLEBEKE 1/10,000

Instructions regarding War Diaries and Intelligence Summaries are contained in F. S. Regs., Part II. and the Staff Manual respectively. Title pages will be prepared in manuscript.

WAR DIARY
or
~~INTELLIGENCE SUMMARY~~.
(Erase heading not required.)

Army Form C.

Place	Date	Hour	Summary of Events and Information	Remarks and references to Appendices
YPRES OPERATIONS	11/8/17		Coy moved to MAPLE TRENCH. NO 3 section arrived 4 30 AM remainder of Coy at 12 noon. No 3 section relieved 4 guns 54th M.G Coy at S.P. I 14 a 32 (Lt Biggs) and I 14 a 49, I 8 c 42 (2/Lt Jones).	
			No 1 section 2 guns (2/Lt Newton) relieved 2 guns 55th M.G Coy at I 13 d 96 and I 14 c 16. 2 guns (Lt Shatter) were attached to 10th ESSEX for operations to take place on 12th inst. These guns took up positions at I 19 b 90 and I 13 d 96.	
			No 2 section (Lt Evans) moved forward & placed one gun at each of the following positions I 13 b 50, I 13 b 31, I 13 b 73 & I 13 d 98.	
			No 4 section moved forward 3 guns (Lt Coates) attached for operations to 6th R. BERKS. and 8th SUFFOLK REGTS. at I 13 b 32 and 1 gun (2/Lt Allan) moved to I 19 b 87.	
	12/8/17		2 Guns in S.P. at I 14 a 32 knocked out by shell fire & relieved by 2 guns of No 4 section from I 13 b 32. Lieut Biggs badly wounded in S.P. I 14 a 32. The operations of 53rd Bde which were to take place today postponed. 169th M.G. Coy relieved our position on LEFT of MENIN ROAD and our gun positions after relief were as follows.	[signature] Capt. O.C. 53rd M.G. Coy

A5834 Wt. W4973/M687 750,000 8/16 D. D. & L. Ltd. Forms/C.2118/13.

Instructions regarding War Diaries and Intelligence Summaries are contained in F. S. Regs., Part II. and the Staff Manual respectively. Title pages will be prepared in manuscript.

WAR DIARY
or
INTELLIGENCE SUMMARY.
(*Erase heading not required.*)

Army Form C. 2118.

Place	Date	Hour	Summary of Events and Information	Remarks and references to Appendices
YPRES. OPERATIONS (Contd)	12/8/17		1 Gun at J13 d 98, 1 gun J19 b 87, 1 gun J19 b 99, J14 c 91, J14 c 21, J13 d 96. The remaining guns were drawn back into reserve.	
	13/8/17		Guns remained in position as for 12th inst.	
	14/8/17		Four guns No 4 section (Lt Coates) from reserve position to J13 b 38 in support of 4th LONDONS. 4 Guns No 1 section to J19 b 87, J13 d 96, J13 d 98, and J14 c 21	
	15/8/17		2 Guns No 3 section from reserve to STIRLING CASTLE in support and 2 guns No 3 section at J13 d 98. Otherwise guns in position as for 14th inst.	
	16/8/17		1 Gun No 3 section moved from J13 d 98 to J14 a 45 & reported to 17th MIDDLESEX REGT. Otherwise guns in position as for previous day.	
	17/8/17		Coy relieved by 193rd M.Gun Coy. Relief complete 8 am & Coy moved back to DICKEBUSCH HUTS. Throughout the operations from 31/7/17 – 17/8/17 Coy sustained few casualties taking into account the very	

A5834 Wt. W4973/M687 750,000 8/16 D. D. & L. Ltd. Forms/C.2118/13.

Ref. Sheet 27. N.W.

Instructions regarding War Diaries and Intelligence Summaries are contained in F. S. Regs., Part II. and the Staff Manual respectively. Title pages will be prepared in manuscript.

WAR DIARY
or
~~INTELLIGENCE SUMMARY.~~

(Erase heading not required.)

Army Form C. 2118.

Place	Date	Hour	Summary of Events and Information	Remarks and references to Appendices
YPRES. OPERATIONS	17/8/17	(Contd)	Heavy enemy shelling. The casualties throughout being 1 off. 11 O.R	
	18/8/17		Entrained at DICKEBUSCH SIDINGS for ROUBROUCK AREA – arrived ROUBROUCK 7.Pm	
	19/8/17		Resting.	
	20/8/17		Cleaning guns, material, refitting.	
	21/8/17		-Do-	
	22/8/17		-Do-	
	23/8/17		Training. 4 hours per day	
	24/8/17		-Do-	
	25/8/17		-Do-	
	26/8/17		Sunday	
	27/8/17		Musketry practice on Range "B" at EPERLEQUES	
	28/8/17		Training.	
	29/8/17		-Do-	
	30/8/17		-Do-	
	31/8/17		Range practice at EPERLEQUES – M.GUN	

A5834 Wt. W4973/M687 750,000 8/16 D. D. & L. Ltd. Forms/C.2118/13.

Identification Trace for use with Artillery Maps.

19 | 20 | 21

13 | 14 | 15

TARGET A

TARGET B

TARGET C

53rd M.G. Battery

TO BE PLACED OVER ZILLEBEKE SHEET. 1:10,000

NOTE. (1). These traces are intended to facilitate the communication of information as to the position of targets, which have been located on a squared map. The squares on this trace are 500 yards in length on the 1/10,000 scale, 1,000 yards in length on the 1/20,000 scale, and 2,000 yards in length on the 1/40,000 scale.

(2). The squares on the trace are fitted to the squares of the map showing the targets, which are then drawn on the trace. Sufficient letters and numbers must also be added to enable the recipient to place the trace in the correct position on his own map. A little detail may also be traced, but this is not essential. The name and scale of the map to which the trace refers must be always given. The trace can be used for the 1/10,000, 1/20,000, or 1/40,000 scale.

G.S.G.S. 3023.

Tracing taken from Sheet ....

of the 1: .... map of ....

Signature .... Date ....

Identification Trace for use with Artillery Maps.

TO BE PLACED OVER ZILLEBEKE SHEET. 1:10,000

NOTE. (i). These traces are intended to facilitate the communication of information as to the position of targets, which have been located on a squared map.

(ii). The squares on this trace are 500 yards in length on the 1/10,000 scale, 1,000 yards in length on the 1/20,000 scale, and 2,000 yards in length on the 1/40,000 scale.

(iii). The squares on the trace are fitted to the squares of the map showing the targets, which are then drawn on the trace. Sufficient letters and numbers must also be added to enable the recipient to place the trace in the correct position on his own map. A little detail may also be traced, but this is not essential. The name and scale of the map to which the trace refers must be always given. The trace can be used for the 1/10,000, 1/20,000, or 1/40,000 scale.

G.S.G.S. 3023.

Tracing taken from Sheet ....

of the 1: .... map of ....

Signature .... Date ....

1

53rd Coy
Machine Gun Corps.

War Diary
for
September 1917

Vol 19

Army Form C. 2118.

Instructions regarding War Diaries and Intelligence Summaries are contained in F. S. Regs., Part II. and the Staff Manual respectively. Title pages will be prepared in manuscript.

WAR DIARY
or
INTELLIGENCE SUMMARY.

(Erase heading not required.)

Place	Date	Hour	Summary of Events and Information	Remarks and references to Appendices
RUBROUCK AREA	1 Feb 1917		Company training	
	2	-	Sunday	
	3	-	Company training	
	4	-	Do. (No 1 section practice attack with Essex Regt)	
	5	-	Do	
	6	-	Do	
	7	-	Long Range (two practices fired)	
	8	-	Company training	
	9	-	Sunday	
	10	-	Company training.	
	11	-	Rehearsal of inspection by Army Commander.	
	12	-	Company training	
	13	-	Long Range (two practices repeated)	
	14	-	Coy training	
	15	-	Do.	
	16		Sunday.	

[illegible signature], Capt.

O.C. No. 53 COY. MACHINE GUN CORPS

A5834 Wt. W4973/M687 750,000 8/16 D. D. & L. Ltd. Forms/C.2118/13.

Instructions regarding War Diaries and Intelligence Summaries are contained in F. S. Regs., Part II. and the Staff Manual respectively. Title pages will be prepared in manuscript.

WAR DIARY
or
INTELLIGENCE SUMMARY.
(Erase heading not required.)

Army Form C. 2118.

Place	Date	Hour	Summary of Events and Information	Remarks and references to Appendices
	1917.			
RUBROUCK AREA	17 Sep.		Brigade Route March. Inspection by Gen Sir Ivor Maxse. Company complimented on its condition & turn out.	
	18	–	Company training	
	19	–	Do.	
	20	–	Do.	
	21	–	Do.	
	22	–	Do.	
	23	–	Moved to new area. Entraining ESQUELBECQ for POPERINGHE thence to Camp at {F.25c.n.d Ref Belgium & France Sheet 27 1/40000} (ROAD CAMP) where Company arrived 1 a.m.	
	24		Company training } also series of lectures at Corps school 24/27 Sept.	
	25		Do.	
	26		Do.	
	27		Do.	
	28		Do.	
	29		Do.	
	30			

[illegible] Capt.
O.C. No. 53 COY. MACHINE GUN CORPS.

A5834 Wt W4973/M687 . 750,000 8/16 D. D. & L. Ltd. Forms/C.2118/13.

52 Machine Gun Coy

Vol 20

War DIARY

for

October 1917

Instructions regarding War Diaries and Intelligence Summaries are contained in F. S. Regs., Part II. and the Staff Manual respectively. Title pages will be prepared in manuscript.

WAR DIARY
or
INTELLIGENCE SUMMARY.
(Erase heading not required.)

(1)

Army Form C. 2118.

Place	Date	Hour	Summary of Events and Information	Remarks and references to Appendices
ST. JANTER BIEZEN	1917 Oct.			
	1		Company training.	
	2		Practice Attack carried out with Batts over training area	
	3		Company training	
	4		Do.	
	5		Practice Attacks repeated	
	6		Company training	
	7		Sunday	
	8		Practice Operations	
YPRES OPERATIONS	9		Company moved to CANAL BANK. Section Officers & N.C.Os reconnoitred forward area.	
	10		Barrage positions reconnoitred. Brigade came into support this day.	
	11		Nos 2 & 3 sections moved up to Barrage positions in V.25a Ref. POELCAPPELLE 1/10000. Nos 1 & 4 sections moved to Assembly positions, where No 4 became attached to the assault & No 1 to Consolidation troops.	
	12		Attack launched at dawn by 55th Brigade, who failed to make good their objectives. Barrage Guns (Nos 2 & 3 sections) were withdrawn to CANAL BANK in the evening. Principally due to weather conditions TD	

A5834 Wt. W4973/M687 750,000 8/16 D. D. & L. Ltd. Forms/C.2118/13.

Instructions regarding War Diaries and Intelligence Summaries are contained in F. S. Regs., Part II. and the Staff Manual respectively. Title pages will be prepared in manuscript.

WAR DIARY
or
INTELLIGENCE SUMMARY.

(Erase heading not required.)

(2)

Army Form C. 2118.

Place	Date	Hour	Summary of Events and Information	Remarks and references to Appendices
YPRES. OPERATIONS	1917 Feb. 12		fact no time was allowed to recover these. The 8 guns fired between 6,000 rounds against a much heavier programme. No 1 Sections withdrew to PALACE FARM in support.	
	13		The two guns attached to 6th R. BERKS assault moved to CANAL BANK on relief of R. BERKS regt. [illegible] H.Q. & Company H.Q. moved also to CANAL BANK.	
	14		8th SUFFOLK REGT relieved & withdrew to CANAL BANK. The two guns attached to this Battn also moved to CANAL BANK. They had suffered nine casualties out of fifteen O.R. The mud & weather conditions had rendered both of these guns unserviceable for immediate work. No 1 Section relieved by 54 Coy came back to CANAL BANK. Total Casualties during above operations 12 O.R.	
	15		53 Brigade relieved 55 in the line. 8 guns relieving 8 of 55 Company.	
	16		Held the line as on previous day.	
	17		Company relieved by 54 M.G. Coy & moved back to CANAL BANK	
	18		Company embussed for TUNNELLING CAMP.	

A5834 Wt. W4973/M687 750,000 8/16 D. D. & L. Ltd. Forms/C.2118/13.

Instructions regarding War Diaries and Intelligence Summaries are contained in F. S. Regs., Part II. and the Staff Manual respectively. Title pages will be prepared in manuscript.

WAR DIARY
or
INTELLIGENCE SUMMARY.
(Erase heading not required.)

(2)

Army Form C. 2118.

Place	Date	Hour	Summary of Events and Information	Remarks and references to Appendices
YPRES	1917 Oct		Practice Assault Arrived at.	
PREPARATIONS	19			
POELCAPPELLE	20		Company entrained for CANAL BANK where orders were received to relieve 52 Coy in the line.	
	21		Line held. 8 Guns assembled to consolidate ground to be won next day	
	22		Attack launched at dawn all objectives gained.	
			Guns (three) which had taken up positions at OXFORD HOUSES where direct fire could be obtained on MEUNIER & CAMERON HOUSES failed to procure early targets owing to mist. A few targets were engaged in the afternoon & dispersed	
			The two guns to assist consolidation of MEUNIER HOUSE came into position in excellent time & without casualties.	
			Several small parties of the enemy dribbling through to CAMERON HOUSE in the afternoon were engaged.	
			Considerable difficulty was experienced in getting the guns for consolidation of the left flank in area of REVELLES FARM.	

A5834 Wt. W4973/M687 750,000 8/16 D. D. & L. Ltd. Forms/C.2118/13.

Instructions regarding War Diaries and Intelligence Summaries are contained in F. S. Regs., Part II. and the Staff Manual respectively. Title pages will be prepared in manuscript.

WAR DIARY
or
INTELLIGENCE SUMMARY.
(Erase heading not required.)

(4)

Army Form C. 2118.

Place	Date	Hour	Summary of Events and Information	Remarks and references to Appendices
YPRES OPERATIONS POELCAPPELLE	22		The Hun obtained a direct hit on assembly pill box killing three & wounding two O.R. & knocking both guns & tripods out of action. Support guns were sent for & two withdrawn from those holding the line. Having reorganized teams no difficulty beyond some heavy shelling at POELCAPPELLE was experienced in bringing the guns into position. Going was extremely heavy in the area of REVELLES FARM	
	23		Orders received that 34 Coy would relieve us in the line. Owing to its being impossible to relieve in the dark arrangements were made to carry this out at dawn the following day. Casualties during this second phase of the operations 2 officers 15 O.R.	
	24		Relief carried out & Coy moved to TUNNELLING CAMP.	
	25/30		Training & recuperation at TUNNELLING CAMP.	

[illegible] Capt.

A5834 Wt. W4973/M687 750,000 8/16 D. D. & L. Ltd. Forms/C.2118/13.

Instructions regarding War Diaries and Intelligence Summaries are contained in F. S. Regs., Part II. and the Staff Manual respectively. Title pages will be prepared in manuscript.

WAR DIARY
or
INTELLIGENCE SUMMARY.
(Erase heading not required.)

53 M.G. Coy

Army Form C. 2118.

Vol 21

Place	Date	Hour	Summary of Events and Information	Remarks and references to Appendices
PEGWELL CAMP	Nov.			
PROVEN	1		Coy training.	
	2		do.	
	3		do	
	4		Entrained at PROVEN for BOESINGHE where Company had dinners & proceeded through to relieve 106 Company in the line. 2 sections (8 guns) in forward area on MAIN DEFENCE LINE. 1 – (4 guns) in support at Coy. H.Q. (SIGNAL FARM). The latter also performing anti-aircraft duties. Relief was completed without event.	
	5/9		Line held. Work carried on at all gun emplacements which were in very poor condition. No event of any importance occurred during this time.	
	10		54 Company relieved us. Our Company moving back to 'H' Camp.	
	11/16		General training & cleaning up. Camp drained & huts	

D. D. & L., London, E.C.
(A7883) Wt. W809/M1672 350,000 4/17 Sch. 82a Forms/C/2118/14

Instructions regarding War Diaries and Intelligence Summaries are contained in F. S. Regs., Part II. and the Staff Manual respectively. Title pages will be prepared in manuscript.

WAR DIARY
or
INTELLIGENCE SUMMARY.
(Erase heading not required.)

Army Form C. 2118.

Place	Date	Hour	Summary of Events and Information	Remarks and references to Appendices
			protected against hostile bombing raids.	
	17		Proceeded to take over from 154th Coy same sector as before	
			2 O.R. Casualties wounded by artillery.	
	18/22		Line held with no event of any importance occurring. Enemy aircraft became more active over forward areas during this period & two VICKERS positions were chosen in the forward area to combat these.	
	23		Relieved by 154 Company & proceeded to BOX CAMP.	
	24/28		[illegible] guns etc.	
	29		Proceeded to take over the old sector. 1 O.R. killed & 5 O.R. wounded by artillery during the relief.	
	30		Line held. 1 O.R. wounded at CINQ CHEMINS	

[illegible] Capt.
O.C. 53rd M.G. Coy.

D. D. & L., London, E.C. (A7883) Wt. W803/M1672 350,000 4/17 Sch. 52a Forms/C/2118/14

Instructions regarding War Diaries and Intelligence Summaries are contained in F. S. Regs., Part II. and the Staff Manual respectively. Title pages will be prepared in manuscript.

WAR DIARY
or
~~INTELLIGENCE SUMMARY.~~
(Erase heading not required.)

53 M G Coy
Vol 22

Army Form C. 2118.

Place	Date	Hour	REF. TRENCH MAP. A1. 1. 10,000 Summary of Events and Information	Remarks and references to Appendices
SIGNAL FM	1/12/17.		Coy holding line.	
	2		-Do-	
	3		-Do-	
	4		-Do-	
	5		Relieved by 54th M.G. Coy. Relief complete without incident. Coy	
BOX CAMP A5c19.			moved back to BOX CAMP.	
	6		Coy reorganising and cleaning up.	
	7		" Training	
	8		"	
	9		Sunday	
	10		Training One section proceeded to line & relieved one section	
			55th M.G. Coy at PASCAL FM and VEE BEND and CANON FM.	
MARGUERITE CAMP	11		Coy moved to MARGUERITE FARM at B9 a 21 coming into support.	
	12.		Training	
	13		Inter-Coy relief at PASCAL FM, VEE BEND and CANON FM.	
	14		Training.	S. R. Pocock [illegible] O.C. 53rd M.G. Coy

D. D. & L., London, E.C.
(A7883) Wt. W803/M1672 350,000 4/17 Sch. 52a Forms/C/2118/14

Instructions regarding War Diaries and Intelligence Summaries are contained in F. S. Regs., Part II. and the Staff Manual respectively. Title pages will be prepared in manuscript.

WAR DIARY
or
~~INTELLIGENCE SUMMARY.~~
(Erase heading not required.)

Army Form C. 2118.

Place	Date	Hour	Summary of Events and Information	Remarks and references to Appendices
MARGUERITE CAMP	15		Coy Training –	
	16		Coy relieved in ~~[illegible]~~ ~~to~~ support area by 172nd M. G. Coy.	
	17		Coy moved back to HERZEELE.	
HERZEELE	18		" Training.	
	19		"	
	20		"	
	21		"	
	22		"	
	23		Sunday. Church Services.	
	24		Coy Training.	
	25		Xmas Day.	
	26		Coy Training.	
	27		"	
PROVEN.	28		Coy moved to RAISTOW CAMP. PROVEN.	
MARGUERITE CAMP	29		" " " MARGUERITE CAMP. ELVERDINGHE.	
	30		" Training.	S.R. Pocock Lieut. O.C. 53rd M.G. Coy

D. D. & L., London, E.C. (A7883) Wt. W809/M1672 350,000 4/17 Sch. 52a Forms/C/2118/14

Instructions regarding War Diaries and Intelligence Summaries are contained in F. S. Regs., Part II, and the Staff Manual respectively. Title pages will be prepared in manuscript.

WAR DIARY
or
INTELLIGENCE SUMMARY.
(Erase heading not required.)

Army Form C. 2118.

Place	Date	Hour	Summary of Events and Information	Remarks and references to Appendices
MARGUERITE CAMP.	31/1/17	–	Coy Training & preparing to take over line on 1/1/18.	

S. R. Pocock. Lieut.
O.C. 53rd M.G. Coy

D. D. & L., London, E.C.
(A7883) Wt. W803/M1672 350,000 4/17 Sch. 52a Forms/C/2118/14

www.ingramcontent.com/pod-product-compliance
Lightning Source LLC
Chambersburg PA
CBHW081354160426
43192CB00013B/2403
9781474510882